101 KEY IDEAS

WORLD

RELIGIONS

As of 12-1-01

Created 2001
Last Act 2005
Catal Chaps 2

101 KEY IDEAS

WORLD RELIGIONS

Paul Oliver

TEACH YOURSELF BOOKS

For UK orders: please contact Bookpoint Ltd, 130 Milton Park, Abingdon, Oxon OX14 4SB. Telephone: (44) 01235 827720, Fax: (44) 01235 400454. Lines are open from 09.00–18.00, Monday to Saturday, with a 24-hour message answering service. Email address: orders@bookpoint.co.uk

For U.S.A. order enquiries: please contact McGraw-Hill Customer Services, P.O. Box 545, Blacklick, OH 43004-0545, U.S.A. Telephone 1-800-722-4726. Fax: 1-614-755-5645.

For Canada order enquiries: please contact McGraw-Hill Ryerson Ltd., 300 Water St, Whitby, Ontario L1N 9B6, Canada. Telephone: 905 430 5000. Fax: 905 430 5020.

Long renowned as the authoritative source for self-guided learning – with more than 30 million copies sold worldwide – the *Teach Yourself* series includes over 300 titles in the fields of languages, crafts, hobbies, business and education.

British Library Cataloguing in Publication Data
A catalogue record for this title is available from The British Library

Library of Congress Catalog Card Number: On file

First published in UK 2001 by Hodder Headline Plc, 338 Euston Road, London NW1 3BH.

First published in US 2001 by Contemporary Books, A Division of The McGraw-Hill Companies, 4255 West Touhy Avenue, Lincolnwood (Chicago), Illinois 60712-1975 U.S.A.

The 'Teach Yourself' name and logo are registered trade marks of Hodder & Stoughton Ltd.

Cover photo from Mike Stones
Typeset by Transet Ltd, Coventry, England.
Printed in Great Britain for Hodder & Stoughton Educational, a division of Hodder Headline Ltd, 338 Euston Road, London NW1 3BH by Cox & Wyman Ltd, Reading, Berkshire.

Impression number	10	9	8	7	6	5	4	3	2	
Year		2007	2006	2005	2004	2003	2002	2001		

Contents

Introduction

Welcome to the **Teach Yourself 101 Key Ideas** series. We hope that you will find both this book and others in the series to be useful, interesting and informative. The purpose of the series is to provide an introduction to a wide range of subjects, in a way that is entertaining and easy to absorb.

Each book contains 101 short accounts of key ideas or terms which are regarded as central to that subject. The accounts are presented in alphabetical order for ease of reference. All of the books in the series are written in order to be meaningful whether or not you have previous knowledge of the subject. They will be useful to you whether you are a general reader, are on a pre-university course, or have just started at university.

We have designed the series to be a combination of a text book and a dictionary. We felt that many text books are too long for easy reference, while the entries in dictionaries are often too short to provide sufficient detail. The **Teach Yourself 101 Key Ideas** series gives the best of both worlds! Here are books that you do not have to read cover to cover, or in any set order. Dip into them when you need to know the meaning of a term, and you will find a short, but comprehensive account which will be of real help with those essays and assignments. The terms are described in a straightforward way with a careful selection of academic words thrown in for good measure!

So if you need a quick and inexpensive introduction to a subject, **Teach Yourself 101 Key Ideas** is for you. And incidentally, if you have any suggestions about this book or the series, do let us know. It would be great to hear from you.

Best wishes with your studies!

Paul Oliver
Series Editor

Allah

Allah is the name given by Muslims for the one true God whose will was revealed by Muhammad and is recorded in the *Qur'an*. Allah is perceived as being transcendent and yet is able to know and understand all aspects of the world and of humanity. Allah is too great to be fully understood by a human being; Allah knows all things. Allah is seen as being the one and only God. For Muslims there is no other God than Allah.

Islam is thus unequivocally monotheistic. There is no place in Islam for any symbolic representations of Allah, so statues or other representations of Allah are very strictly forbidden. The authority, the will and the influence of Allah affect all of life. In other words, Islam and Allah are all-encompassing, affecting each and every aspect of human existence. The logic of this has led to Islamic teachings and principles being integrated in Muslim countries into all facets of society, including the judicial and legal systems, the educational system and the political system. Allah is described as merciful and compassionate, and Muslims feel that Allah is protective towards them. Muslims also submit to the will of Allah in the sense that they regard Allah as being all-wise and all-powerful. Besides being merciful, God is also a dispenser of justice. To those who sin yet repent, then Allah will be inclined towards mercy and forgiveness.

The concept of Allah is central to the first of the Five Pillars of Islam, which are the five principal obligations of all Muslims. The first Pillar of Islam is the Profession of Faith or *Shahadah*. This is that 'There is no God except Allah, and Muhammad is the Messenger of God.' This is the fundamental statement of faith for all Muslims. It is repeated several times each day by Muslims and is also part of the words used by the *muezzin* when he calls the faithful to prayer at the mosque.

> ### see also...
> *Islam; Mecca; Mosque; Muhammad*

Anglican Communion

The Anglican Communion is the group of churches in different parts of the world which are affiliated with the Church of England. The latter is the established church of England.

The Archbishop of Canterbury is accepted as head of the Anglican Communion, although he has no legal function outside England. There are a total of 38 Christian churches which are members of the Anglican Communion, and many of these are in countries which are former British colonies. Examples of member churches are the Protestant Episcopal Church of America and the Episcopal Church of Scotland. One of the unifying features of the Anglican Communion is that every ten years Anglican bishops meet at the so-called Lambeth Conference. This is essentially a means of discussing contemporary Christian issues.

Anglicans accept the ministry of bishops, priests and deacons; the significance of the *Bible* as holy scripture; and the practice deriving from the *Book of Common Prayer* of 1662. The General Synod, first established in 1970, is the decision-making forum for the Church of England. The General Synod has three so-called 'Houses': the Bishops, Clergy and Laity. The Synod is chaired by the Archbishop of Canterbury and the Archbishop of York. It is able to make laws relating to issues about the Church of England.

Besides the provinces of Canterbury and York, there are a total of 44 dioceses under the administration of bishops. An important issue for the Anglican church in recent years has been the ordination of women. The General Synod approved the principle of the ordination of women in 1994, and later that year a number of women priests were ordained.

see also...
Christianity; Methodist Church; Roman Catholic Church

Asceticism

There is a long history in many religions of adherents denying themselves, to varying degrees, the material pleasures of life in order to help them focus upon a life of spirituality. Such self-denial may range from the avoidance of eating certain types of food, to retreating in solitude to an isolated place.

The general assumption behind asceticism is that serious spiritual advancement will tend not to be found among the physical and material pleasures of daily life. Christian asceticism started relatively early, and at least by the third century CE. The early ascetics established themselves in the deserts of Egypt, and many of them led solitary lives. Some lived in caves, while others developed fairly extreme forms of asceticism based upon physical endurance. Gradually communities of ascetics developed which were in many ways the forerunners of the medieval monastic tradition. Both Basil the Great in Turkey, and Martin of Tours in France, established religious communities in the fourth century CE.

In India there is a very long tradition of asceticism ranging from the *munis* of the *Vedas*, to the anonymous sages who wrote the *Upanishads*. There are also the present-day sadhus, sannyasins or wandering holy men, who are still a common sight in India. Historically, although orthodox religious authority within Hinduism resided with the Brahmin priestly caste, the sannyasin represented an alternative route to spiritual knowledge which could be described as mystical. Sannyasins may live in the forest or a cave and practise meditation and yoga. The essential attribute of Hindu ascetics is that they should relinquish all material possessions and support from the family, devoting themselves to a life of meditation and contemplation of God.

see also...

Hinduism; Jainism; Sadhu

Baha'i

The Baha'i religion is considered by its adherents to be a universal world religion. It is a revealed religion and began in present-day Iran in the nineteenth century.

The original founder of Baha'i was Mirza Ali Muhammad who was born in 1820. He assumed the name 'The Bap' and considered himself to be in the tradition of leading religious figures such as Jesus and the Buddha. One of his followers was Mirza Husain Ali (1817–1892) who assumed the name Baha'u'llah. He considered that he was the medium through which God was able to reveal Himself on earth. In a sense he considered that Baha'i was the flowering of other world religions, or alternatively that other religions consisted of a preliminary phase of development of Baha'i.

Baha'u'llah asserted that the purpose of his revealed faith was to help introduce a new moral order to the world, which was a reflection of the ethical position of other world faiths. Baha'is would help to provide a coherence and unity for the religious aspirations of humanity. In a sense,

Baha'i developed in an Islamic environment, but Muslims have been very keen to repudiate Baha'i. Muslims generally consider Baha'i to be an unacceptable deviation from the faith of Islam.

The general Baha'i philosophy is to strive for a unified world, in which people live a cooperative and peaceful life. The Baha'is generally feel that people may not understand some aspects of other religions. Baha'i may be able to clarify these matters and lead people to a new unified vision of God. The Baha'is are very much concerned with social issues, and believe that the development of unitary political and economic structures for the world can assist in the development of a moral world society.

see also...
Non-violence

Baptism

Baptism is one of the Christian sacraments. It is the process whereby someone enters the Christian church. The act of baptism usually involves the person being completely or partly immersed in water, or perhaps having some water placed on the head. Sometimes the priest may make the sign of the cross on the head with water. The baptismal rite usually also involves the pronouncement of a form of words involving the Holy Trinity – God as Father, Son and Holy Spirit. In the Anglican and Roman Catholic Churches, baptism usually takes place when the individual is a baby, but some traditions such as that of the Baptists, argue that only adult baptism is appropriate. They suggest this because they feel that only when people have reached a certain degree of maturity are they able to understand fully the significance of joining the Christian Church.

The original concept of baptism involved complete immersion in water, but fairly rapidly in the history of the church, the process of baptism by pouring water three times over the head was seen as acceptable. The significance of the water used in baptism is that the sacrament involves a process of spiritual cleansing. Normally water from a stone font is used. The parents and godparents of the baby are present as the priest sprinkles water over the baby's forehead.

Baptists, who believe in the process of complete immersion, take the new church member into a purpose-built pool as a symbol of spiritual cleansing. In churches practising infant baptism, there may be a later process of confirmation. This is the ceremony at which an older individual affirms that s/he wishes to be a member of the church, and the bishop confirms his/her membership.

---

see also...

Anglican Communion; Christianity; Holy Trinity; Roman Catholic Church

Benares

Benares is arguably the holiest city to Hindus, and is situated in the state of Uttar Pradesh to the east of Allahabad. It is also known as Varanasi, or Kashi – the city of light. The city is bounded on three sides by rivers; the Varuna to the north, the Assi to the south, and the Ganges to the east.

Benares is perhaps most famous for the *ghats*, or stone steps which lead down to the river Ganges. Religious people come to the *ghats* to pray and meditate, to practise yoga, and, in particular, to immerse themselves in the Ganges, which is regarded as an important act of devotion. It is also reputed that anyone who dies and is cremated on the banks of the Ganges at Benares, achieves *moksha* or release from the cycle of birth and death. Hence, many of the *ghats* are given over to cremation of the dead. The Manikarnika Ghat is the principal cremation site. The corpses are burned in wood fires and the remains then scattered in the Ganges.

To the north of Benares is Sarnath, where the enlightened Buddha preached his first sermon in the deer park. It was there that he met the five ascetics whom he had known previously, and who, having heard the teachings expounded by the Buddha, became his disciples. To the south of Benares is the famous Benares Hindu University. This was founded in 1892 as the Central Hindu College at Benares by Annie Besant, the theosophist and socialist. In 1916 it was given a university charter, and there was an opening ceremony attended by the Viceroy, Lord Hardinge. Mahatma Gandhi made a famous speech during the ceremony in which he commented upon the nature of British rule in India, and also upon some facets of Indian society.

see also...

Hinduism; Moksha; Salvation; Siddhartha Gautama

Bhagavad Gita

The *Bhagavad Gita* is a relatively short spiritual poem which is part of the very much longer Hindu epic, the *Mahabharata*. It is possibly the widest read of Hindu scriptures. The poem opens with two large armies facing each other; but many of the combatants face a dilemma as there are warriors on opposing sides who are related to each other. Arjuna, a leader of one of the armies, surveys the scene and does not wish to fight. He feels that whatever wealth or power he might gain, it would not be worth having to fight and perhaps kill his relatives. Arjuna confides in his charioteer, who happens to be Krishna, the eighth incarnation of the Hindu god Vishnu. The remainder of this poem of 18 chapters is devoted to Krishna's advice to Arjuna, partly in relation to this specific dilemma, but also in relation to spiritual matters and the conduct of human life in general.

The opening chapter of the *Gita* which describes the above scene can, of course, be taken literally, and one can read Krishna's advice as if set within this particular context. However, the *Gita* is widely interpreted as an extended metaphor, the opening chapter referring to the kind of ethical dilemmas which face all human beings during their lives. In the latter case, the *Gita* can be read as advice on the conduct of human existence. Krishna's basic message to Arjuna is that he should fight, but this can easily be interpreted as meaning that human beings should fight against wrong, and stand up for what they see as right.

In Chapter 3, Krishna outlines the more general doctrine of *karma yoga*. He argues that human beings cannot avoid acting in the world, and indeed they should act, but in a special kind of way. They should always act in as moral a way as they see fit, but should not be concerned with what they might gain from their actions.

see also...

Bhakti; Hinduism; Krishna; Vishnu; Yoga

Bhakti

In Hinduism, this is the tradition of practising devotion to a personal god. The god, perhaps Vishnu or Shiva, displays grace for the individual human being, and through a combination of human devotion and God's grace, human beings are released from *samsara*, the cycle of rebirth. They thus attain *moksha*, or release.

Devotion to the chosen god may be demonstrated in the temple or in the home. Hymns may be sung, prayers offered, and flowers and food may be placed before the statue of the god. *Puja* is the term used for the process of making prayerful offerings to a deity. The statue of the god may be treated rather like a human being. The feet may be washed, and bells rung and music played for the deity. The acts of devotion to God are essentially individualistic, and hence there is little difference in religious significance in worship conducted at the temple or at home.

The Bhakti tradition arguably developed most clearly in southern India, particularly in the Tamil-speaking areas. The tradition evolved in the ninth and tenth centuries CE, and developed further under Ramanuja who was born in the eleventh century. While Ramanuja conceded that knowledge and understanding of God were important precursors for salvation, the most appropriate approach for human beings was the way of devotion, or *bhakti yoga*. Devotees should place their trust entirely in God, and God would reward them with the gift of grace. Ramanuja's concept of bhakti was that there was a mutually supportive relationship between the devotee and God. The devotee offered love to the deity, and the latter exercised care and protection of the human being.

see also...

Bhagavad Gita; Hinduism; Shiva; Vishnu

Bible

The *Bible* is the scriptural text for the Judaic-Christian tradition, and includes the *Old Testament*, the *New Testament* and the *Apocrypha*. The *Old Testament* spans the period from a description of the creation of the universe, until about 400 BCE. The first five books are sometimes called the *Pentateuch*. The *New Testament* is believed generally by Christians to represent the completion of the prophecies which were made in the *Old Testament*. It has four main divisions. There are the *Gospels*; the *Acts of the Apostles*; the *Epistles* and *Revelation*.

The *Apocrypha* means 'hidden things' in Greek. There are 12 books which were probably written originally in Alexandria. Different versions of the *Bible* have adopted different approaches to the *Apocrypha*. In the *Vulgate Bible*, for instance, they are included with the *Old Testament*. The Council of Jamnia in about 100 CE, established the authorised content of the *Old Testament*. The content of the *New Testament* was finally agreed by about 300 CE.

For many years the *Bible* was regarded as being literally true, but gradually, as scientific understanding developed, it was realised by most people that there would need to be some degree of harmonisation between science and the *Bible*. The first translation of the *Bible* was made by St Jerome in the fourth century CE and was into Latin. William Tyndale was the first to translate the *Bible* into English. There was considerable opposition to the work of translation in England, and hence Tyndale had to move to continental Europe. His translation of the *New Testament* was printed in 1525, but he was not able to complete his translation of the *Old Testament*. Accused of heresy, he was arrested and executed in 1535.

see also...

Christianity; Judaism; Scripture

9

Buddhism

Buddhism is the religion founded by Siddhartha Gautama who was born near Lumbini, in what is now southern Nepal in about 536 BCE. After being reared in relatively affluent surroundings as a prince, Siddhartha relinquished his family and social status, and became a wandering religious mendicant. After undergoing various religious disciplines, Siddhartha achieved a spiritual enlightenment while undergoing a lengthy period of meditation.

After this experience, he was known as the Buddha or enlightened one. He then travelled to Benares where he delivered a sermon which outlined his fundamental teaching in terms of the Four Noble Truths and the Noble Eightfold Path. The Buddha established a community of monks and nuns, and had a long period expounding his teaching until he died in about 483 BCE.

Although the image of the meditating Buddha is very familiar, and indeed is given a central place in Buddhist temples and monasteries, it is not the object of worship. The Buddha himself is revered as a great spiritual teacher, but the central aspect of Buddhism are the teachings of the Buddha which have been passed on by a combination of oral and written traditions.

After the Buddha's death there was a doctrinal division, and there developed two main 'schools' of Buddhism. The Theravada tradition is found today primarily in South-east Asia, while the Mahayana tradition developed in Tibet, China and Japan. Despite doctrinal differences the central message of Buddhism remains the same. The Buddha provided a way which was intended to help the individual escape from suffering, by being non-attached to the world of the senses, and by letting go of the feelings, whether favourable or unfavourable, which arise within human beings.

see also...

Buddhist meditation; Four Noble Truths; Noble Eightfold Path

Buddhist meditation

The process of meditation is central to Buddhist practice. It is used in the first place to calm the mind in order to help the individual be receptive to spiritual practice; and second, to gain insight into the real nature of the world. This latter process leads ultimately to the attainment of enlightenment, a condition in which the person is no longer deluded by any aspect of life, but sees into the true nature of existence.

In Buddhist monastic communities, it is the custom to meditate at fixed times of the day, usually in the early morning and in the evening. Meditation may be accompanied by chanting of extracts from appropriate scriptures, and by the use of mantra. It is the tradition when meditating to sit in the lotus posture with legs crossed, although other postures, such as kneeling or sitting upright in a chair, are also suitable. There are now many opportunities in western countries for laypeople to receive instruction in meditation from monks and nuns in monasteries.

In the Theravada Buddhist tradition meditation usually commences with practice designed to still the mind through contemplation of the breath. The mind is focused upon the steady inhalation and exhalation of the breath, often by sensing the air as it passes the tip of the nostrils. The main purpose of such meditation is to focus upon a steady calming object, and the breath is simply one which may be chosen. The aim is to help the mind attain a tranquil state which is not unduly disturbed by random thoughts. This type of meditation involving focusing upon the breathing is termed *anapanasati*.

When the mind has reached a stable state, the person can begin to explore the nature of ideas which arise in the mind. This type of meditation is known as *vipassana* meditation.

see also...

Buddhism; Dukkha; Four Noble Truths

Caste system

About 2,000 years BCE, the extensive plains of central southern Asia were inhabited by nomadic peoples who organised themselves into various tribal groups. They maintained large herds of horses and engaged in small-scale agriculture. These so-called Aryan people were impelled by a variety of possible factors to migrate southwards towards India, and in a series of invasions spread over time, gradually conquered northern India.

The Aryans already had a social hierarchy, and perhaps not surprisingly this was imposed on the indigenous people of India. By the early part of the first millennium BCE, four main social classes were crystallising in Indian society. The most influential class were the Brahmins, followed by the Kshatriyas, the Vaishyas and the Shudras. The original Sanskrit word for these social classes was *varna*.

The Brahmins were the theocracy of ancient India. They were priests whose fundamental role was to study and memorise the scriptures, and to make sacrifices in the temples. As Hinduism gradually developed from the original Aryan religion, the Brahmins became more and more powerful in society, as they were the principal means of mediation between ordinary people and the gods. Inevitably, to some extent, spiritual power encouraged the development of political and economic power.

The Kshatriyas were the princes, secular rulers and warriors. They were politically influential. The Vaishyas were principally traders, business people and farmers. They acted as the mainstay of the economy. The role of the Shudras was essentially to serve the needs of the higher three classes. As Hinduism developed, the four main classes went through a gradual process of subdivision based primarily upon occupational groupings. These subdivisions are more accurately referred to as castes.

see also...

Hinduism; Karma; Moksha; Sanskrit; Vedas

Christianity

his is the religion founded by Jesus Christ. Christianity developed within a historical context of Judaism, and inherited some concepts from that faith. The *New Testament* contains a record of the teachings of Jesus as they have passed down to us, but to some degree the doctrinal basis of Christianity has evolved over the years.

Christianity is monotheistic, and asserts that God is three individuals in one : the Trinity of Father, Son and Holy Spirit. Christians claim that Jesus Christ was the son of God. Some early Christians believed that Jesus was the Messiah, or leader who had come to help the Jews to conquer their enemies. Christians view God as having been made Man in Jesus, who then suffered, died and was resurrected. The spiritual power of God is often referred to as the Holy Spirit. Christians believe that Jesus atoned for the sins and wrongdoing of mankind by his suffering and death on the cross. People should have faith in Jesus, and then, according to Christians, they will achieve salvation. The soul is considered to exist after death, and may go to a realm of happiness where God exists, i.e. Heaven, or to a place of eternal unhappiness, i.e. Hell. The well-known figurative language and symbolism associated with these concepts has had a very significant effect upon Christians over the centuries.

Worship is an important element in Christianity and can take many different forms. These may include prayer, chanting, singing of hymns, meditation and the eucharist. There have, in the last two centuries, been a number of critiques of Christianity, arising largely from the development of scientific understanding. Nevertheless, Christianity has been very influential in terms of its impact on western society. Ethical values deriving from Christianity, including an emphasis upon the equality of human beings, have tended to encourage social reform.

see also...
Jesus; Scripture

Christmas

Christmas is the anniversary of the birth of Jesus Christ, and is one of the major festivals of Christianity. In the early development of Christianity, it is likely that Christians did not celebrate Christmas. The actual date of the birth of Jesus was not known, and there was disagreement about the most appropriate date to hold the festival.

In some parts of the Roman Empire the festival of Christ's birth was held on January 6, but gradually December 25 came to be the accepted date. By the middle of the fourth century CE, the celebration of Christmas on December 25 had become largely recognised. This date was probably chosen because it is the original non-Christian festival of the Winter Solstice. There had been a Roman festival on this date dedicated to the sun and celebrating the lengthening of the day in preparation for spring.

The religious element of Christmas is clearly one of giving thanks for the birth of Jesus, as described in the gospels of the *New Testament*. A link is also sometimes made between the humble nature of his birthplace in a stable, and the elements of the teachings of Jesus which support the poor and disadvantaged.

There are a large number of customs which have developed around Christmas, which derive from both Christian and non-Christian sources. The Saturnalia of Roman times, held on December 17, was a time of giving each other gifts. Nowadays, presents for children are associated with St Nicholas, a fourth-century bishop who has become the patron saint of children, and also given rise to the characters of Father Christmas and Santa Claus. The customs of Christmas such as the holly and the ivy, and log fires, all have non-Christian origins.

see also...

Christianity; Church; Easter; Festivals; Jesus

Church

The word 'church' can be used in several senses. It can, of course, simply signify a building devoted to Christian worship; or it can be used in the sense of 'the Christian Church' meaning the collective community of those who believe in the message of Jesus Christ. The word church derives from the Greek *ekklesia*, meaning a gathering of people of the same belief.

The Christian Church is sometimes termed 'catholic', which means that it is worldwide. In other words even though there may be different denominations with slightly different patterns of worship, they all belong to the same church with belief in the teachings of Jesus. The adjective 'apostolic' is sometimes attached to churches. This indicates the adherence to the teachings of the *New Testament* apostles.

Churches as Christian buildings do differ somewhat depending upon the particular denomination, and even within denominations. In a church typical of the Church of England, there will be an altar with a cross at the front of the church. A carved wooden pulpit is used for the preaching of sermons, and a lectern for supporting the *Bible* when read. Usually at the west side of the church there may also be a carved stone font for holding water when children are baptised. In a Roman Catholic church there may be a statue of the Virgin Mary in a fairly prominent position, and at the high altar will typically be six candles and a crucifix.

An Orthodox church may look relatively more ornate. In front of the altar there may be a large screen termed an iconostasis, on which are religious paintings. Quakers, or the Society of Friends, do not have churches as such. The buildings in which they meet are very simple, and members usually sit on benches or chairs arranged approximately in a circle.

> ### see also...
> *Christianity; Methodist Church; Roman Catholic Church*

Confucianism

For much of the history of China, Confucianism has been the principal philosophy and state-sponsored religion. It was founded by Confucius, or Kung Fu-tzu, to use his original name. Confucius was born in 551 BCE in northern China, and died in 479 BCE.

Confucianism has a very strong practical ethical dimension, and relatively less emphasis on formal religious observances. To a certain extent, then, it may be regarded as a guide to human conduct and inter-personal relations, rather than a religion in the commonly accepted sense. It could perhaps be described as a religious approach to life. There is a considerable emphasis upon social cohesion, with family unity being regarded as the basis for the social solidarity of the broader society. To this end, Confucianism encourages family members to respect each other, and for the ruler of a state to exert compassionate authority, while citizens are loyal to the ruler.

Confucianism places considerable emphasis upon human beings acting with empathy towards each other,

and in this lies a significant religious element. Confucianism is in many ways a very practical religion. It places very little emphasis on other-worldly concerns. The principal concern is how human beings live their lives and relate to others, rather than a preoccupation with a deity.

Confucianism places great stress on human beings trying to understand their own relationship with the world and also with others. The feeling is that this kind of understanding is essential before the individual can attempt to understand the nature of God and the possibility of life after death. Confucianism is very much concerned with maintaining the norms and values of society, and of supporting the existing social structures.

see also...

Taoism

Covenant

The term covenant is found particularly in Judaism and refers to a special kind of agreement between God and the Jews. Essentially a covenant is an agreement, both religious and moral, which places certain obligations upon the Jews, and which also stipulates certain consequences if the agreement is not kept.

There are several different covenants referred to in the *Old Testament*, but two of the principal ones are those between God and Abraham, and God and Moses. In the *Book of Genesis* God appears to Abraham in a vision and promises to protect him. God promises Abraham that he will have many descendants, among whom will be kings and rulers of people. Moreover, this covenant promised by God is declared by Him to be an everlasting covenant, applicable to all the subsequent generations after Abraham. The covenant between God and Abraham was to be marked by the the act of circumcision of all males. Should a male not be circumcised, then that man would not be part of the covenant with God.

A second important covenant is described in the *Book of Exodus*, after Moses has led the Israelites out of Egypt. The Israelites camp in the Sinai desert, at the foot of Mount Sinai, and God calls Moses up onto the mountain, explaining to him the basis of the covenant. God says that if the Israelites will abide by the covenant, then they will be held by God in the highest esteem, above all other people. The Israelites agree with Moses that they will keep God's covenant. God then spells out the terms of His covenant. The first condition is an emphasis upon strict monotheism, and an injunction against worshipping statues of other gods. The remainder of the Ten Commandments is also outlined. The nature of such covenants has given the Jewish people a sense of identity and of relationship with God.

see also...

Judaism; Sabbath; Synagogue; Talmud; Torah

Dharma

This term exists in two forms i.e. *dharma* in Sanskrit, and *dhamma* in the Pali language of Theravada Buddhism. The fundamental meaning of dharma is the moral and spiritual order which pervades the universe. Everything in existence is affected by dharma, and the latter may be thought of as the prime causal factor in the existence of all living things.

In classical Hinduism this led dharma to be thought of as the general principle which should be used as a guide by people in how to behave. Hence dharma had a normative function, and one which was subtly different for individuals of different social classes. In a related sense, dharma also became the basis of civil law, in that it prescribed acceptable forms of behaviour.

In Buddhism, dharma or dhamma is used as a synonym for the teachings of the Buddha. The argument here is that the concept of dharma involves a notion of a naturally existing spiritual order, and the purpose of the Buddha's teaching was to make that order or spiritual force clear to all people. Within a Buddhist framework, when people recognise the validity of the dharma, they will act in accordance with it. Hence dharma is also used as a term to describe the characteristics of moral behaviour which are in accord with Buddhist precepts.

For Buddhists dharma can be thought of as the fundamental reality of the universe. In a sense, dharma is present in everything, and the purpose of human beings is to attempt to live in the present, and to attune themselves to the dharma. Buddhists speak of practising dharma, by which is indicated the intention of trying to live according to the advice given by the Buddha, and hence to live in accord with the truth of the nature of the world.

see also...

Buddhism; Hinduism

Diaspora

The word diaspora comes from the Greek meaning dispersion, and normally refers to the phenomenon of the many Jewish communities living around the world away from Israel. The notion of the diaspora started in 586 BCE when the Babylonians, having overcome the Kingdom of Judah, forcibly removed many Jews to Babylonia to work as slave labour. Although this would have been an extremely difficult period for the Jewish captives, they succeeded in maintaining their own culture and religion. Synagogues were built as a focus for religious practice. Eventually Babylonia itself was conquered by the armies of Cyrus the Great of Persia, and Cyrus allowed those Jews who wished, to return to Judea from 538 BCE onwards. It is probable however, that some Jews elected to remain in Babylonia. Under the Roman Empire, a great many Jews lived throughout the empire. A particularly important community was that in Alexandria. Inevitably, to some extent, Jewish communities absorbed the language and culture of the countries in which they lived.

The creation of the state of Israel has in a sense, focused the minds of Jews on the diaspora, and upon the extent to which Jews should try to return to Israel. Some Jews hold the view that those living in the diaspora will inevitably lose much of their culture, and lose contact with their religious traditions.

In general terms, Orthodox Jews tend to support the return of Jews to Israel. Reform Jews, in contrast, generally feel less strongly about this, tending to the view that a legitimate Judaism can be sustained within the diaspora. Nevertheless there is a widespread consciousness of Israel within the diaspora. Some Jews feel that the ultimate purpose of all Jews should be to return to Israel, while others consider that modern Israel does not give the pre-eminence to traditional Judaism that it should.

The word diaspora may also be used to refer to the dispersion of other peoples from their homeland.

---

see also...

Judaism

Disciples

A disciple is a follower of a religious teacher. The term tends to be used of a person who is a follower or student of a particular individual, rather than someone who is an adherent of a religious faith.

As religions have become organised there is a tendency for people to be followers of the religion rather than of individuals within it. Hence, in the present day, one would tend only to find the term used in religions where there is still the tradition of following individual teachers. This occurs in Hinduism for example, where it is still common for a young man in say, his teens, to attach himself to a teacher or guru. There will then follow a period of discipleship of as much as ten years, during which the disciple will learn aspects of yoga, meditation and prayer. At the end of this period of studentship, the disciple will normally become an individual teacher in his own right, and perhaps take students of his own.

Disciples usually act as advocates for the teaching of their tutor, and to some extent disseminate those teachings. They also help to ensure the continuity of the teachings after the teacher's death. The student is usually attracted to a teacher by a combination of the quality of the teaching and also by the personal magnetism of the individual.

The term is used more specifically of the followers of Jesus Christ. The 12 disciples formed the nucleus of the followers of Jesus, and they had a significant role to play in some of the key moments of the life of Jesus. In any religious tradition, it is no small matter for a person to give up his or her normal life, and follow a religious teacher. When it is recorded in the gospels that James and John left their father Zebedee in his boat to follow Jesus, one may conjecture that it was difficult for them to abandon their family obligations to follow the religious life.

see also...

Hinduism; Jesus

Divinity

The word divinity has the same derivation as the Latin for god, and refers literally to the study of those elements in society which are regarded as divine, holy, spiritual or godlike. Regarded as a subject, it is very similar to theology. Indeed, some university departments use the term divinity to mark out an area of study.

Divinity as a subject area can perhaps be distinguished from religious studies: the former tends to be applied within the context of a specific religious tradition such as Christianity. Strictly speaking, within the context of the derivation of the term, one would hesitate to use it in relation to a faith such as Buddhism which does not incorporate the notion of a deity. Both divinity and theology would therefore tend to be employed for religions where there was a clear concept of a divine being. Religious studies, by the same token, would typically embrace the study of any system which had religious elements. One might argue that it could reasonably include the study of yoga and meditation, even when they are decontextualised from a particular religion such as Hinduism.

There is another important distinction which could be made between divinity and theology on the one hand, and comparative religion and religious studies on the other. The former tends to be used within a conceptual framework where the basic tenets of a religion are not formally challenged. In other words, the religious concepts may be discussed, analysed and contrasted, but generally within the framework of an accepted belief system. In the discipline of religious studies, however, there are fewer, if any, concepts which are accepted as 'given' in terms of their accepted truth or validity. Religious concepts, for example, may be subjected to sociological analysis, in an attempt to show that they have evolved within a particular set of social circumstances.

see also...

Christianity; Hinduism

21

Dukkha

In the Buddhist tradition dukkha is the concept of suffering. On one level the entire purpose of Buddhism can be seen as the attempt to eliminate suffering from human existence. However, this should not be misunderstood through the assumption that Buddhism seeks to eliminate all the things which may result in suffering such as illness, death, parting from people we love, and the general misfortunes of life. Buddhism seeks to transform the attitude of people to such events, in order that they do not respond to them by suffering. Buddhism tries to develop in people a new type of consciousness which enables them to view such things in a different way, so that they do not experience dukkha.

Siddhartha Gautama is reputed to have left his palace as a young man, and to have seen an old person, a sick person, and a dead person. This was in some ways the starting point of his understanding of suffering. Until that time he had led a very sheltered and comfortable existence, and had not appreciated the extent of suffering in the world. This prompted him to begin his spiritual quest which was to lead to his own enlightenment.

Buddhists argue that most people, from time to time, acknowledge to themselves that human existence is impermanent and will end in death. However, they attempt for the majority of their lives to forget such unpleasant thoughts, and to create the most pleasant environment for themselves. In short, they try to create happiness or *sukha*.

Buddhists would argue that this strategy, while it may help in the short term, is fundamentally flawed. The unpleasant feelings associated with dukkha will eventually return. Buddhists suggest that people should not simply try to replace suffering with happiness, but instead analyse the nature of suffering itself.

see also...

Buddhism; Impermanence

Easter

This is the Christian festival which remembers the crucifixion and resurrection of Jesus Christ. The date of Easter has never been fixed in the same way as that of Christmas, and Easter may currently occur between March 22 and April 25. Preceding Easter Day are the 40 days of Lent, and following Easter are the 40 days leading up to Ascension. As with Christmas, many traditions of Easter are derived from the non-Christian past. The word Easter has evolved from the Anglo-Saxon word for the Goddess of Spring, Eostre. Easter eggs reflect a pre-Christian celebration of fertility. It is possible that originally eggs were not eaten during the period of Lent, and hence became symbolic of the creation of life, and therefore of the resurrection of Jesus. It is also possible that the hare, which was in ancient times associated with fertility, has given rise to the myth of the Easter bunny which brings eggs for children.

Easter is one of the most ancient of the Christian festivals, and gives a focus to the Christian calendar of worship. Originally Sunday was the day of the remembrance of the crucifixion and resurrection, but this has now been transformed from a weekly celebration to the single annual festival of Easter.

In the early stages of the development of the Christian Church, when people wished to be baptised, this was usually conducted at Easter. Hence, it was during Lent that people intending to be baptised were prepared for the significance of the ceremony. The week before Easter is usually described as Holy Week, and begins on Palm Sunday which is the Sunday before Easter Sunday. Palm Sunday recognises the event when Jesus rode into Jerusalem on a donkey. Crosses made out of palm leaves are distributed to the congregation on Palm Sunday.

see also...

Christianity; Jerusalem; Jesus; Resurrection

Festivals

Religious festivals fulfil a number of interrelated functions. They are usually events in which members of the religious community participate, and hence build up a sense of group solidarity. Festivals are also usually connected in some way with the central or key events in the development of a faith.

Easter is an example of a Christian festival which remembers the crucifixion and resurrection of Jesus. On Good Friday there are services in churches which remember the passion of Jesus, and which provide an opportunity for Christians to meditate upon the suffering which Jesus experienced on the cross. The remembrance on Good Friday of a sad event is replaced by the optimism of Easter Sunday and the realisation that Jesus is not dead. Candles are lit during Easter Sunday services to symbolise the resurrection.

The festival of Holi is a well-known Hindu celebration. It takes place in March and celebrates at least partly the legend of the baby Krishna killing a demon. The characteristic feature of Holi is that everyone throws powdered paints and coloured water at each other.

In India, Sikhs follow many of the traditional Hindu festivals, particularly the components of them which are cultural rather than specifically religious. There are several important Sikh festivals, particularly significant being those held on the birthdays of Guru Nanak and Guru Gobind Singh, and also on the date on which Guru Arjan was executed. These festivals are known as *gurpurbs*. They may typically involve the *Guru Granth Sahib* being transported on a ceremonial stand through the local town, and also a large communal meal. Another event which often takes place at festival time is a reading of the *Guru Granth Sahib* in its entirety.

see also...

Christianity; Hinduism; Sikhism; Worship

24

Four Noble Truths

The historical Buddha, Siddhartha Gautama, was brought up in a very privileged position for the society of his time. He was born into the ruling family of a small kingdom in the southern part of what is now Nepal. Although he led a relatively comfortable and luxurious life, the young Siddhartha was curious about life outside the secluded palace grounds. One day, according to tradition, he set out and came across an old person, a diseased person and a corpse. He was apparently shocked by this, as he had been sheltered from the less pleasant side of human existence. Finally, he saw a Hindu ascetic who was seeking spiritual understanding. This experience awakened Siddhartha to the unsatisfactoriness of existence. He appreciated for the first time that life must end in illness and death.

He determined to leave the palace to become a wandering ascetic and to seek an understanding of how people could cope with this phenomenon of suffering. Having subjected himself to a discipline of strict meditation and self-denial, he eventually gained an insight into how one might understand and be at peace with the reality of suffering. This is termed enlightenment.

After this event he journeyed to Benares and in the nearby deer park preached his famous sermon of the Turning of the Wheel of the Law. The core of the sermon is contained in the so-called Four Noble Truths. These are, first, that suffering exists; second, that there is a cause for that suffering; third, that it is possible to counteract that suffering; and fourth, the Buddha outlined a strategy to achieve this. The Buddha argued that suffering was caused not so much by the experiences in life, but by the human desire for life to be pleasant. He suggested that it was in principle possible for human beings to learn to lose such desire, and hence cease to suffer.

see also...

Buddhism; Buddhist meditation; Noble Eightfold Path

Fundamentalism

In religious terms fundamentalism is a perspective on belief which tends to attribute absolute authority and truth to the original sources of the religious knowledge in question. Such sources may be religious revelations which have been transmitted orally or in writing. Fundamentalism is characterised by a general unwillingness to interpret such sources in the light of more recent scholarship. The original ideas and cornerstones of faith are seen as immutable, and there should not be an evolution in their interpretation.

In Christian terms, fundamentalism often involves an unchallenging belief in the absolute truth of the *Bible*. As Biblical scholarship developed there was a tendency to interpret the *Bible* in terms of the widening understanding of the social and political milieu of the times. Fundamentalism would generally hold that the received content of the *Bible* should be given pre-eminence rather than attempting to interpret it in the light of historical analysis. There is also a general rejection of the application of scientific experimentation and analysis to Biblical understanding. Hence fundamentalism would tend to accept the account of creation in the *Book of Genesis*, rather than any account based upon Darwinian evolution.

Fundamentalism in religious contexts has tended to arise when, rightly or wrongly, it was perceived that the religion as originally revealed or understood was declining in some way. Hence, there would be a call for renewing the religion in terms of its first principles.

Perhaps it is reasonable to expect that all faiths should have a traditionalist element in their development. Nevertheless, fundamentalism does raise issues about the extent to which religious revelation should be seen as absolute knowledge, or whether all knowledge, including the religious, is relative to the particular social context in which it arises.

---

see also...

Bible; Christianity

Gandhi

Gandhi's full name was Mohandas Karamchand Gandhi, although he was known as Mahatma Gandhi, a term which means 'great soul'. This is indicative of the spiritual content of Gandhi's approach to life. He was born in Porbandar in the state of Gujarat into a family of devotees of the God Vishnu, and who were also to some extent influenced by Jainism. Perhaps the latter was one of the causes of Gandhi's lifelong interest in and commitment to vegetarianism. When, as a young man, he left India for England to study at the Inns of Court in London, he continued with his vegetarianism although it was somewhat difficult in the London of the time. Vegetarianism was also to some extent part of his commitment to *ahimsa*, or non-violence to living things.

When Gandhi, now a qualified barrister, moved to South Africa, he was deeply affected by the prejudice shown against Indians. Even though he himself was subjected to violence, he always advocated peaceful resistance. He urged his supporters to show their disagreement and non-acceptance of unfair and discriminatory policies, but always advised them to do so in a completely peaceful manner. Equally well they should, according to Gandhi, always adhere to the truth as they saw it.

Gandhi's dignified behaviour in South Africa, even when provoked, led some of his political opponents to express their respect for him. Gandhi had friends and colleagues from all cultural and religious groups, and he argued that all the main world religions were fundamentally true. Nevertheless, he adhered primarily to Hinduism, and in particular he tried to abide by the teachings contained in the *Bhagavad Gita*. Gandhi established *ashrams* or religious communities in both South Africa and India. In the conflict with the British in India in the 1930s and 1940s, he consistently applied his religious philosophy of non-violence and adherence to truth.

> ### see also...
> *Bhagavad Gita; Hinduism;*
> *Non-violence*

Golden Temple

The Golden Temple is a large temple complex in Amritsar in Panjab, northern India. As a building, it is the main focus of the Sikh religion. It is also sometimes called the Harimandir Sahib or the Darbar Sahib. The fourth Sikh guru, Ram Das, first established Amritsar as the centre for Sikh worship and started to construct the town. He arranged the digging of a large water tank there. The fifth guru, Arjan, continued the construction of Amritsar, and under his administration it became an important regional centre.

Perhaps significantly, the foundation stone of the Golden Temple was laid by a famous Muslim mystic, Mian Mir. This is an indication of the respect which Sikhs had always paid to other religions from the time of Guru Nanak. In fact, when Guru Arjan was compiling the *Adi Granth* he included the writings of two Muslim saints. One significant feature of the Golden Temple is that it has a door on each of the four sides, which is a symbolic representation of the Sikh religion being open and receptive to individuals of all faiths and castes.

The Hindu tradition in India had been to enshrine religious knowledge in the Brahmin caste, and to some extent this had resulted in social stratification and the accumulation of wealth and secular power by the Brahmins. Guru Nanak had criticised this social system, stressing that all people were equal before God. Women also were not necessarily treated equally in Indian society and the Sikh tradition had tried to rectify this. The building of doors on four sides was an attempt to stress this philosophy of social inclusion in Sikhism.

In 1604 the newly compiled Sikh scripture, the *Adi Granth*, was placed in the Golden Temple by Guru Arjan. The sixth guru, Hargobind added a building to the Golden Temple complex called the Akal Takht, which functioned as a focus for decision making for social and political issues among the Sikhs.

> ## see also...
> Sikhism

Gurdwara

The gurdwara is the building used by Sikhs for collective worship and community events associated with religion. It is the focus of all cultural events within the Sikh community.

A typical gurdwara usually consists of the same main functional areas. There is a prayer hall, a communal kitchen and eating area, an entrance foyer in which shoes are left on entry, and one or two small additional rooms which may be used for religious instruction or the teaching of Panjabi. The prayer hall may be on the upper floor of the building, and is carpeted wall to wall. At one end of the hall the *Guru Granth Sahib*, the holy scripture of the Sikhs, is placed. It is positioned on a raised dais over which is an ornate frame and canopy. During worship a *chowri* is periodically waved over the holy book as a mark of respect. The *chowri* consists of a bundle of yak hair fixed into a handle.

On entering the prayer hall everyone sits on the floor, men on one side and women on the other. This separation is of cultural rather than religious significance, as Sikhs have always emphasised the equality of people in all respects, including both gender and caste. Part of the significance of sitting on the floor is that people are at a lower level than the *Guru Granth Sahib* and hence show respect.

The *langar* or kitchen has both symbolic and practical importance. In the Hindu society in which Sikhism developed, there were many restrictions related to caste in terms of the preparation and consumption of food. Members of one caste might be forbidden from eating with members of a different caste. When worship in the prayer hall is completed, a communal meal is served. The notion of everyone eating together emphasises the equality of all.

> **see also...**
>
> *Golden Temple; Guru Granth Sahib; Sikhism*

Guru

In the Hindu tradition a guru is a religious teacher, originally a teacher of the *Vedas*. A guru would accept several young students and would instruct them in the meaning of the sacred scriptures, and ensure that they learned certain important parts of the *Vedas*. In exchange for the instruction and guidance, the students would minister to the needs of the guru, perhaps cleaning the house, fetching water, and if necessary begging for food alms.

The guru normally did not charge for the tuition provided. Some gurus have been very well known and have founded religious communities with many disciples. Examples are Sri Ramakrishna, Swami Narayan and Sai Baba, all of whom were active in the nineteenth century and whose organisations are still influential today. Other gurus, however, are simply religious individuals, whether wandering sadhus or resident teachers, who take on a disciple.

The student will receive tuition in yoga, meditation, religious ceremonies and the scriptures. The student may remain in contact with family and parents, visiting them occasionally. Primarily, however, the guru will take care of his student, acting as a replacement parent. Eventually the student will part from his guru, perhaps taking on his own student. The relationship between guru and student remains forever, and from time to time the student will visit the guru to reinforce, in a sense, his religious life.

In the Sikh religion the concept of the guru is central to the faith. It can signify, first, God as guru; or second, the historical ten Sikh gurus who interpreted the word of God, and finally the *Guru Granth Sahib*, or *Adi Granth*, which is the holy scripture and represents, in written form, the word of God. The Sikh religion is monotheistic, and God is the ultimate guru and source of spiritual truth.

see also...

Disciples; Guru Granth Sahib; Hinduism; Sikhism

Guru Granth Sahib

The *Guru Granth Sahib* is the religious book of the Sikhs. It is regarded as representing the word of God and is treated with enormous respect. In the prayer hall of the gurdwara (Sikh temple) it is regarded as an object of devotion, and is placed on a decorated stand under a canopy. In order to demonstrate their respect for the book, members of the congregation sit on the floor, below the level of the *Guru Granth Sahib*.

The holy book contains the religious writings of six of the Sikh gurus and also of a number of saints and poets. Thus it contains the work of Guru Nanak, Guru Angad, Guru Amardas, Guru Ramdas, Guru Arjan and Guru Tegh Bahadur. It has also the works of Kabir, Farid and Bhai Gurdas. The *Guru Granth Sahib* is, therefore, a compilation of the work of a number of writers, and it was prepared by the fifth Guru, Arjan, who lived at Amritsar. Bhai Gurdas worked as an assistant to Guru Arjan, and under his guidance. The holy scripture was placed in the Golden Temple in Amritsar in 1604. The inclusion of poets and mystics other than Sikh gurus in the holy book is an indication of the general tolerance of Sikhs. Kabir, for example, worked as a weaver in Benares, but established a reputation among ordinary people as a religious mystic and teacher. Farid lived in Panjab and was a Muslim, yet his works were still included.

Guru Arjan was unconcerned about both the formal religious affiliation of people, and their caste. What was more important were their devotion and spiritual insights. The poetry and hymns of the *Granth* are arranged in 31 sections, each defined by a particular *raga* or classical Indian melody. Within each *raga* the hymns of Guru Nanak are placed at the beginning, followed by those of the other gurus in chronological sequence.

see also...

Golden Temple; Gurdwara; Guru Nanak; Sikhism

Guru Nanak

uru Nanak was the founder of the Sikh religion and was born in Panjab in northern India in 1469 CE. He was born in a town called Talwandi (located now in the Pakistani part of Panjab) and his father worked for the local ruler of the area. The family was Hindu and hence Nanak was brought up within a Hindu culture, and received a good educational grounding in Sanskrit and Persian. He is reputed to have been somewhat withdrawn and thoughtful as a child.

When he was about 16 he was married to Sulakhni, and two sons were born to them, Sri Chand and Lakhmi Das. Nanak, however, did not adapt easily to married life, and showed little inclination to retain steady employment. It was clear that he had very strong religious and mystical leanings, and at this period he tended to avoid human society and meditate and pray on his own. For a short time he lived in the area of Sultanpur, and it was from here that he embarked on a series of long religiously inspired journeys. He travelled for a period of about 25 years. Nanak visited a number of places of Hindu pilgrimage including Hardwar and Benares, and travelled as far as Bengal in the east and Sri Lanka in the south. He is said also to have travelled to the Himalayas, and outside India to Afghanistan, Iran and Arabia.

When he eventually returned to Panjab he witnessed the invasion of India by Babar. It is suggested by some sources that he was imprisoned at this time, but later released. He lived in his later life at the village of Kartarpur where he founded a spiritual centre (*dharamsala*). Before he died he appointed his successor who became known as Guru Angad. Nanak died in 1539 CE. In founding the Sikh religion, Guru Nanak emphasised certain key principles of the moral and religious life. He criticised an excess of ritual in religion, and argued against the social effects of the caste system.

see also...

Gurdwara; Guru Granth Sahib; Sikhism

Hajj

The Hajj is the name of the pilgrimage to Mecca that every adult Muslim is expected to make at least once during a lifetime. The focus of the journey is the shrine of the Kaaba in Mecca. The Hajj is the fifth of the Five Pillars of Islam. Part of the purpose of the Hajj is to reinforce the sense of community and solidarity with all other Muslims which is engendered by mixing together in close proximity during the pilgrimage.

The Kaaba is a black cube-shaped shrine which according to tradition was built by Ibrahim and his son Ismail. In one corner of the Kaaba is a large black stone which was given to Ibrahim by the angel Gabriel. The Kaaba is connected with the life of Muhammad, for when he marched into Mecca, he destroyed the statues which had been placed in the Kaaba, thus emphasising the monotheistic nature of Islam.

The Hajj takes place each year between the eighth and 13th days of the 12th month, Dhu al-Hijjah, of the Islamic calendar. The first stage of the Hajj is when individuals prepare themselves spiritually for the pilgrimage. Men leave aside their normal clothing and wear two white sheets, while women wear a long white dress or one made from plain material, and also wear a covering on the head.

The next stage of the Hajj is to travel to the Great Mosque in Mecca. The people then walk around the Kaaba in an anticlockwise direction seven times. Pilgrims next travel to the Plain of Arafat about 25 kilometres away, and stand from midday to sunset in contemplation and prayer to Allah. Afterwards they travel to Mina near Mecca, where they throw stones at three stone pillars which symbolise the devil. Finally there is the festival of Id ul-Adha at which animals are sacrificed.

see also...

Allah; Islam; Mecca; Muhammad; Pilgrimage

Hindu temple

Hindus tend to divide their acts of worship between the home and the temple, and indeed many acts of prayer and devotion take place at a shrine in the home. The shrine may consist of a shelf on which there is a statue of a god such as Krishna, and perhaps also paintings of the god in question. There may also be a lamp for burning butter or *ghee*, and various bright decorations. Offerings of flowers and fruit may be placed before the statue at times of worship. The temple fulfils the function of providing communal worship and may also be a focus for community activities.

Temples have a variety of different structures and among the Hindu community of the United Kingdom a variety of buildings have been used for temples. In this case there is no particular structural pattern. Typically, however, a temple has an inner shrine room with the principal statue of the deity to whom the temple is dedicated. The priest will attend this deity, dressing the statue in ornate clothes and ensuring offerings of food are present. Lamps may be lit before the statue and incense burned. Leading up to the statue will be a more open area where visitors and devotees sit. Here there may also be statues of religious figures and also religious paintings. The door of the temple which leads into this large area will often face eastwards.

The statue of the deity may be treated rather like a human being in that early in the morning the priest may symbolically wash and dress the figure, and in the evening again wash it before the deity sleeps for the night. During the presence of the congregation the priest may well initiate an *arti* ceremony in which candles or lamps are lit before the deity. Prayers or readings from the *Vedas* take place and the lamps are then passed round the people present.

see also...

Bhakti; Hinduism; Krishna; Sanskrit; Upanishads; Vedas

Hinduism

This is the principal religion of India, although the Indian population also numbers many followers of Islam, Jainism, Christianity and other religions. In addition to being a religion Hinduism can also be considered as a complex social system which is embedded within Indian society. The well-known existence of social classes and castes is an example of the close connection between the religious and the social aspects of society.

Hinduism is not a revealed religion in the sense of having a single founder, but evolved from the interaction between the Aryan invaders of India in the second millennium BCE, and the indigenous inhabitants. The priests of the Aryans recited a series of hymns known collectively as the *Rg Veda*, and portions of this are still in use by traditional Hindus today.

Although Hinduism is characterised by a multiplicity of gods and goddesses such as Krishna, Rama, Sarasvati, and Ganesha, it can, perhaps paradoxically, also be seen as a monotheistic religion. Many Hindus focus their religious thought on Brahman, the ultimate spiritual force of the universe. At the same time they may offer devotion to a more personal god who may be regarded as a manifestation of the absolute. Hindu families will often maintain a small shrine in their homes, devoted to a personal god, where they will perform acts of *puja*. This may involve prayer, contemplative thought and the placing of offerings such as flowers and food before the shrine. Such devotion to a god is known as *bhakti*. Hinduism is an extremely varied religious tradition, and whereas many other major religions have a certain uniformity of practice, this is much less evident in Hinduism.

The ultimate purpose of all Hindu religious practice is *moksha* or release from the cycle of reincarnation, and therefore ultimate union with God.

see also...

Hindu temple; Krishna; Shiva; Vishnu; Yoga

Holy Communion

Holy Communion is the form of Christian worship in which bread and wine are distributed to the congregation. This act of worship is known variously as the Eucharist, the Mass, and the Lord's Supper as well as Holy Communion. It is a reminder of the Last Supper which Jesus ate with his disciples, at which bread and wine were consumed. At that meal Jesus attached special significance to both bread and wine, referring to the former as his 'body' and the latter as his 'blood'. The bread and wine have become symbols for Christians, reminding them of the crucifixion and then resurrection of Jesus. For some Christians the bread and wine act as a means of remembering Jesus, while for others Jesus is regarded as present in spirit during the communion service.

Individual churches have a different approach to the significance of the eucharist. In the Roman Catholic and Anglican churches there is a general belief that Jesus is present in the bread, and the latter is hence known as the 'host'. The priest will say prayers in front of the bread and wine, and this is termed consecrating them. There is the assumption then that the spirit of Jesus is present. The doctrine of transubstantiation suggests that even though the bread and wine do not change in appearance during the act of consecration, they do actually become in a sense the body and blood of Jesus. This doctrine is accepted by Roman Catholicism. The term 'eucharist' means thanksgiving and is a means of giving thanks for the sacrifice made by Jesus in giving his life, and also for the resurrection.

The eucharist appears to have developed at an early stage in the history of the Christian church. By 150 CE the pattern of worship on Sundays was becoming established, and the sharing of bread and wine seen as a symbol of the passion of Jesus.

see also...

Anglican Communion; Christianity; Jesus; Roman Catholic Church

Holy Trinity

This is the Christian concept that God interacts with human beings in three fundamental ways. First of all God is perceived as the Father, the all-powerful and all-knowing deity who created the universe. Second, God is seen as present on earth in the person of Jesus Christ, the Son of God, who redeemed the sins of mankind. Third, God is perceived as being present in and among human beings as the Holy Spirit, the spiritual power which is a tangible force for good in the world.

The doctrine of the Holy Trinity has raised interesting theological questions for the Christian Church through the ages, notably the issue of how to reconcile this doctrine with the monotheism of the Christian tradition. There is in the *New Testament* an implicit suggestion of the doctrine of the Trinity, but the latter was developed over the early centuries of the Christian Church.

It was at the Council of Nicaea in 325 CE that a measure of agreement was reached on how a single God could be conceived as the three persons of Father, Son and Holy Spirit. In the *New Testament* Jesus is noted as referring to God as 'Father', and this has provided one basis upon which Christian believers can conceptualise their own feelings towards God. The debate about the relationship between God, and God as Father, Son and Holy Spirit has led Christians to evaluate the concepts of God as completely transcendent, and God as imminent. The concept of God as Son is equally complex and has taxed theologians. One concept is that Jesus was a human being into which the divine spirit had entered. An alternative view was that Jesus was in some way a divine entity who had passed to earth and then assumed a human form in order to be able to teach and influence the affairs of mankind. Christians believe that God also exists as Holy Spirit, and is able to be present in people as a spiritual power.

see also...

Christianity; Church; Holy Communion; Jesus; Prayer

Impermanence

This is one of the central concepts of Buddhism and is often referred to in Buddhist literature using the original Pali word *anicca* (pronounced aneecha). Buddhists regard impermanence as one of the key features of existence.

It is perhaps most clearly evident in the living world, where organisms are born, live for a period, and then die. Yet even when living things are in an apparently stable condition, they are in a constant process of change. Cells are dying and others are being created; the organism is continually adapting to a changing environment. In the human mind too, thoughts arise spontaneously, stay in the mind for a while, and then pass out of consciousness. Thus there is impermanence in the mental world too. In the non-living world of earth and rocks, erosion ensures that little stays the same for long.

In meditation Buddhists often focus upon the breathing, in order to calm the mind. Here, too, there is continuous change, with the rhythmic inhalation of breath, followed by exhalation. As long as we are living, this cyclical process never stops.

Buddhists often contemplate the idea of *samsara* – the wheel of birth and death; the arising and falling away of all things.

For Buddhists, however, it is not so much the phenomenon of impermanence which is important, but the significance of this for our state of mind. Buddhists argue that human beings tend to become very attached to things. People become attached to possessions, to money and to the things it can buy. People become attached to the world of appearances, to things which are seen as pleasant and beautiful. They forget that these are temporary, ephemeral qualities. Inevitably, argue Buddhists, attachment to things which are impermanent brings unhappiness and suffering.

> ### see also...
> *Buddhism; Dukkha; Four Noble Truths; Nibbana*

Islam

slam is one of the major religions of the world, and the word means submission to the will of God. The teachings of Islam were, according to Muslims, revealed to the prophet Muhammad, and later compiled into the Islamic holy scripture, the *Qur'an*. Historical and cultural factors have resulted in a degree of variety in Muslim society around the world, but one can identify certain features of common practice which are known as the Five Pillars of Islam.

Perhaps the most central aspect of being a Muslim is the affirmation of faith in the one God, Allah, and in Muhammad as the messenger of God. Islam is strictly monotheistic, and holds Muhammad as an exemplar for humanity. Second, Muslims offer prayers to God five times each day. Prayers should be said while the individual is facing Mecca, and the prayer times are at daybreak, midday, mid-afternoon, sunset, and evening. Immediately prior to praying, the individual should ritually wash the hands, face and feet. Friday midday prayers are traditionally said in a mosque, led by an imam who also delivers a sermon. The third pillar of Islam is the giving of alms. This is known as *zakat*, and consists of payment of about two and a half percent of an individual's assets and income. The *zakat* is used to support disadvantaged members of the community, and also for teaching about Islam. Fourth, during the ninth month of the Islamic year, Ramadan, Muslims are expected to fast. This is a considerable physical discipline, particularly in many Muslim countries with a hot climate, where individuals must go without food and drink from sunrise to sunset. At the end of Ramadan is the feast of Id ul-Fitr. Fifth, there is the obligation to carry out a pilgrimage to Mecca. This is known as the Hajj, and unless there are special reasons, each Muslim should participate in the pilgrimage at least once in a lifetime.

see also...

Allah; Hajj; Mecca; Mosque; Mohammad; Qur'an

Jainism

Jainism is the Indian religion founded by Mahavira. Jainism is not a theistic religion, but does place great emphasis upon the attainment of salvation. It subscribes to the law of karma and assumes that if one does not act ethically adverse karma will attach to the soul. The only way to escape from the cycle of rebirth is to lead a moral life linked to renunciation of the world. The soul may then attain *nirvana*.

Jainism assumes, however, that the discipline to attain salvation is so strict that only people living in a monastic environment can achieve it. The lifestyle of the Jain monk is very strict. When joining the monastic order, the monk's hair is pulled out hair by hair, rather than having the head shaved. The monastic lifestyle includes periods of fasting and of meditation.

Monks are not supposed to own anything and they must abstain from eating meat and also from killing anything. Jain monks take enormous care to avoid the possibility of killing living things. They typically filter drinking water to save microscopic animals, and wear a piece of gauze over their mouth to avoid inhaling any small organisms. Similarly, when they walk along, they carefully brush the pathway to avoid treading on insects.

Laypeople also subscribe very much to this philosophy of non-violence. They do not engage in farming because tilling the soil may involve killing animals in the earth. Jain laypeople have a tradition of becoming involved in business and in banking. Even laypeople lead a very serious and devout life. They try to be very careful in terms of becoming attached to material things, and devote part of every day to the practice of contemplation and meditation.

see also...

Hinduism; Mahavira; Non-violence; Salvation

Jerusalem

Jerusalem is the capital city of Israel. It is regarded as a holy city and an important place of pilgrimage by Jews, Muslims and Christians.

For Jews the most holy locations include the Temple Mount and the Western or Wailing Wall. For Muslims, Jerusalem is the third holiest place on earth, and a pilgrimage to the city is regarded as a significant religious event. Of particular importance to Muslims are the Dome of the Rock and the Al-Aqsa Mosque. For Christians, there is the Church of the Holy Sepulchre which is built at the assumed location of the burial and resurrection of Jesus.

The site of Jerusalem has been inhabited for between 2,000 and 3,000 years BCE. In 1005 BCE King David established rule over the city, and his son Solomon built the first temple in 969 BCE. In 586 BCE Nebuchadnezzar, the king of Babylon destroyed Jerusalem, and many Jews were exiled to Babylon. A Roman army under Pompey took the city in 63 BCE. The Temple of Jerusalem is one of the most important historical features of the city. After the temple built by Solomon was destroyed by Nebuchadnezzar, it was eventually rebuilt, by Herod the Great among others. Both the First and Second Temple were constructed on the same stone platform, the Temple Mount. The western wall of the Mount is known as the Wailing Wall and is holy to the Jews.

The Dome of the Rock is the Jerusalem mosque, constructed in 691 CE by the tenth Caliph, 'Abd al-Malik. It is built on the same rock as the Temple of Jerusalem. The city was conquered by the crusaders in 1099 CE, but was captured by Saladin in 1187 CE. The Turks ruled the city from 1516 CE and the city walls were rebuilt. In Jerusalem is located the Jewish National and University Library which has the largest collection of works on Judaism in the world.

see also...

Christianity; Islam; Judaism; Mosque; Pilgrimage

Jesus

hristians believe that Jesus was the Son of God, who revealed to humanity a set of religious principles for life which reflected the will of God. He was born in Bethlehem in Judea, but his teachings were delivered in the area of Galilee. His father was a carpenter who was presumably involved in a variety of construction work in the locality. It can be assumed that Jesus was trained in this kind of work by his father, although, in addition, he would probably have received some formal tuition in Jewish history and religion. In adulthood Jesus was baptised by John the Baptist and from that time onwards embarked on a period of preaching and teaching.

Jesus and his disciples led an itinerant life, travelling about the countryside, where Jesus gave religious teaching and also healed people who were ill. In a poor society where there would be little medical treatment, the presence of someone who could heal apparently incurable illnesses must have had a dramatic effect on people. In his teachings Jesus also used examples which would have been within the practical experience of his audience, and hence would appear relevant. Although he could potentially have inherited reasonable financial security from his family, he appears to have rejected material security in life, for what was, in effect, the lifestyle of a homeless religious teacher. He moved across the strata of society, particularly acting as an advocate for those who were less advantaged.

The claims of Jesus to be the Son of God disturbed the Jewish priestly classes, who regarded such claims as blasphemous. After his crucifixion, the body of Jesus was placed in a tomb, but two days later it had disappeared. Later Jesus appeared to his disciples, and they concluded that he had risen from the dead. The resurrection of Jesus became a central tenet of Christian belief.

see also...

Christianity; Church; Disciples; Holy Trinity

Judaism

Judaism is the faith of the Jewish people and is arguably the oldest of the monotheistic religions. The words Judaism and Jew are derived from Judah, the fourth son of Jacob, and in the *Old Testament* one of the 12 tribes of Israel was named after him. It is not easy to produce an all-encompassing and accurate definition of Jews today. One may speak of a Jewish race, although this is not an entirely adequate term given the historical dispersal of Jews around the world. There is not really a religious cohesion since there are individuals who would describe themselves as Jews and who yet share few if any of the traditional convictions of Judaism. It is also not easy to associate Jews simply with the state of Israel, since there are more Jews living outside Israel than within its boundaries.

Judaism is based upon the concept of a transcendent deity who is all-powerful. God is seen as the creator of the universe, but, moreover, who has a special relationship with the Jewish people. This notion derives from Abraham and the covenant made with God, who would henceforth look after the Jewish people, and who in turn would be faithful to God.

The will of God is described in the *Torah*. This was the revelation of God to Moses. When the Jewish people were escaping from Egypt and were resting in the Sinai desert, Moses went up a mountain to pray and meditate upon God. There the Ten Commandments and other laws of God were revealed to him, later to be written down in the *Torah*. Orthodox Jews try to abide by the tenets of the Jewish *Bible*. They believe strictly in the one God who created the universe, and in the covenant with Abraham which relates to all Jews to this day. They also try to apply strictly the laws contained in the *Torah*. A current movement to amend some traditional Jewish practices is known as Reform Judaism.

see also...

Covenant; Diaspora; Jerusalem; Synagogue; Torah

Karma

The doctrine of karma is an intrinsic component of Buddhism, Hinduism and Jainism. The doctrine probably first evolved at the time that the *Upanishads* were being written in India, and involves the idea that the quality and morality of the actions in which people engage in one existence affect the nature of their lives in another life. In other words, karma is very much linked with the doctrine of reincarnation and the transmigration of souls. Karma is regarded as an inescapable law of the universe. If one acts in an unethical fashion then one simply cannot escape the consequences of that action. Unpleasant behaviour to people will at some time in the future, in another reincarnation, result in unpleasant consequences for the person who initiated the behaviour. Therefore, karma passes on with the human soul, as it transmigrates through *samsara*, the wheel of reincarnation.

It has been suggested that the doctrine of karma implicitly supports the caste system in India. If the nature of one's present existence depends upon the manner in which one has behaved in previous lives, then in a sense it can be argued that everyone deserves their present fate. Within this model it may be suggested that those experiencing misfortune deserve such a fate, and equally that those with a fortunate life deserve this also. Karma could thus be seen as justifying a system of social stratification. Within Jainism the doctrine of karma is not entirely different. It is assumed that karma becomes attached to the soul, and thus transmigrates with the soul. Within Theravada Buddhism the term 'rebirth' is used rather than reincarnation, primarily because it is assumed that there is no identifiable soul which migrates from existence to existence.

Nevertheless, the law of karma is regarded as very significant in the lives of people. Karma is a reminder that people should act mindfully in accordance with Buddhist precepts and will thus go some way to avoiding suffering.

see also...

Buddhism; Hinduism; Jainism

Khalsa

The khalsa is the community of Sikhs who have formally committed themselves to the faith. The khalsa members are regarded as equal among their peers. The origin of the khalsa can be dated to 1699 CE when Guru Gobind Singh, the last of the Sikh Gurus, convened a large gathering of Sikhs at Anandpur. For various socio-political and religious reasons he probably considered it important to establish a formal condition of membership of the Sikh community. The Guru spoke to the assembled crowd and said that as a mark of devotion to the Sikh faith and cause, he wanted a volunteer who was willing to be beheaded as a mark of faith. After a period of hesitation a man stepped forward. The Guru took him into his tent and emerged a few moments later with his sword stained red. He then asked for another volunteer and the process was repeated. He continued asking for volunteers until the process had been carried out five times. After this, to what one assumes was the astonishment and relief of the crowd, he brought out the five volunteers completely unharmed. He introduced them to the crowd as the five people on whom the khalsa would be built, and named them the five Beloved Ones.

After this the Guru established a ceremony which is in effect the initiation ceremony for khalsa members. Sugar crystals were added to water in an iron bowl and stirred with a sword to dissolve them. This sugar solution is termed *amrit*, and has given its name to the ceremony termed 'the Amrit Ceremony'. The five men and the Guru drank some of the *amrit*. From that time onwards khalsa members were to signify their membership as Sikhs in five ways. They wore *kesh*, or uncut hair kept in place by a *kangha* or comb. An iron bracelet or *kara* is worn on the wrist, and a *kirpan* or sword is carried. (Today, Sikhs only carry a small token *kirpan*). Finally, *kaccha* or shorts are worn as an undergarment. These symbols are known as the five Ks, since the words all begin with K in Panjabi.

see also...

Sikhism

Krishna

Krishna is one of the *avatars* or incarnations of the God Vishnu. The legend of Krishna probably has its origin in a variety of sources, and today Krishna is one of the most popular deities in Hinduism. The stories of Krishna cast him in a variety of roles including hero, herder of cattle, lover and child. His consort is usually depicted as Radha.

The myth of Krishna usually includes the following key elements. He was reputedly born at Mathura, his mother and father being Devaki and Vasudeva respectively. Krishna and his brother Balarama were forced to escape persecution at the hands of Kamsa, the ruler of the region, and were protected and reared by a cattle herder named Nanda. He is often portrayed during his youth as leading a relaxed rural life, and having continual affairs as the lover of the young female cow herders. Krishna eventually killed Kamsa and then moved away from his home area to establish and rule over his own territory. Later in his life his capital city was subject to fighting between different power groups, and Krishna lost both his son and his brother Balarama.

Eventually, while taking refuge in a nearby forest, Krishna was shot in the heel by an arrow, and died from his wounds. The character of Krishna is well known as the provider of advice to Arjuna in the *Bhagavad Gita*. Krishna is often portrayed as having light-blue skin and playing the flute. The latter is because of the association with being a herder of cattle in his youth.

It has been suggested that Krishna playing the flute and his music inspiring girls to dance with him is a metaphor for the divine music whereby God calls the devoted to Him. Krishna is also a subject in literature a well-known example being *Gita Govinda* written by Jayadeva. This poem focuses upon Krishna's love for Radha and dates from the twelfth century.

see also...

Hindu temple; Hinduism; Shiva; Vishnu

Mahavira

Mahavira, a name which means 'Great Hero', was the founder of the Jain religion in India. His real name was Vardhamana, and he was born in about 540 BCE, which means that he was some 20 years younger than the Buddha. His father was king of the Jnatrika clan in present-day Bihar, and his mother the sister of the king of the Licchavi clan. He was brought up in a privileged environment, but apparently wished to live the life of a religious mendicant.

He initially joined a group of mendicants termed Nirgranthas. With this group he led the life of a sadhu, going on pilgrimages to holy places, practising yoga and meditation, begging for food alms, and debating religious questions with other sadhus and with laypeople. During this period he decided to discard his clothes and walk naked, as do some groups of sadhus today. After about 13 years of this lifestyle he attained enlightenment. Having acquired a growing number of followers and disciples attracted by his teaching, Mahavira embarked on a life as a spiritual teacher which lasted until he died in about 486 BCE.

After his death there eventually arose something of a doctrinal division in Jainism. A shortage of food on the Gangetic Plain resulted in a group travelling to establish themselves in the Deccan area of India. These adherents retained the practice of nudity, while the Jains remaining in the north took to wearing white cotton clothes.

Despite the differences in conduct the essential teaching of Mahavira appears to have been retained by both groups. One of the key features is that the universe is not directed by a supreme deity, but rather operates in harmony with natural laws. Essentially, the universe operates in cycles, rising to a zenith and then declining, each cycle taking many thousands of years.

see also...

Hinduism; Jainism; Non-violence; Siddhartha Gautama

Mantra

A mantra is a short syllable or a phrase of varying length which is regarded as holy. Mantras are normally repeated over and over again. They are used particularly in Hindu and Buddhist religious practices, although elements of related practices can be found in many religions. Mantras vary in their use. They may be employed as prayers and acts of devotion, and also within meditation and yoga. As part of meditation, the usual purpose of repeating the mantra is to steady the mind, and help it to focus purely upon the syllable. In this way the mind does not move backwards and forwards between thoughts, and become deviated from its main spiritual purpose.

Some people have been well known for the use of a particular mantra. Mahatma Gandhi used the syllable *Ram*, a Hindu name for God. The mantra was on his lips at the moment of his assassination. Perhaps the most famous mantra is the syllable *aum*, which derives from the *Upanishads*. The word has a plurality of meanings, among which is an affirmation of the existence of God, Brahman, or an ultimate spiritual power behind the universe. The Sanskrit symbol for *aum* is found in many different Hindu contexts. It is also the opening syllable of a longer mantra, the Gayatri mantra, which is very commonly repeated by Hindus. The Gayatri is part of the *Rg Veda*, and is repeated at all significant events in Hindu religion and culture. It was spoken to the God of the Sun, and may be approximately translated as, 'Let us reflect on the wonder of the god Savita; may our souls be lifted by his power and light.'

In Tibetan Buddhism there is another famous mantra which is written approximately phonetically as, 'Aum mani padmay hum.' It may be translated as 'aum, the jewel in the heart of the lotus', and can be thought of as referring to the ultimate reality in all existence.

see also...

Buddhist meditation; Upanishads; Vedas; Yoga

Mecca

Mecca is the city in Arabia in which the prophet Muhammad was born in 570 CE. In the sixth century CE, Mecca was a very important trading centre. It was situated approximately half way between the northern and southern points of the Red Sea, and at the crossroads of important caravan trade routes between the Arabian Sea, the Persian Gulf and the Mediterranean. Mecca was a tribal society and the pre-eminent tribe was the Quraysh. The tribe was the socio-political entity to which people saw themselves belonging. There were agreements between the tribes which ensured the security and continuity of the trade routes. Mecca contained the Kaaba which according to tradition was built by Ibrahim and Ismael, and before the time of Muhammad contained many statues of the tribal gods. The Kaaba was regarded as holy throughout Arabia and hence Mecca was, in the early sixth century CE, a place of pilgrimage. The tribe of Quraysh were the custodians of the Kaaba and also ensured proper facilities for pilgrims.

The pre-Islamic temple in Mecca was a focal point for both religious and political activity in Arabia. Mecca was the city in which Muhammad's grandfather was the leading political force. When his grandfather died Muhammad was looked after by his uncle. After Muhammad received the revelation of God which is enshrined in the *Qur'an*, he began to preach the message of God to the citizens of Mecca. Some people accepted the Islamic teaching, while others were opposed to it. There followed a period of intense persecution of the young Islamic community.

Muhammad and his followers finally had to flee from Mecca, and settled in Medina. There Muhammad continued to preach the message of Islam, gaining converts and establishing some of the Islamic customs such as the fast during the month of Ramadan. Eventually Muhammad was able to re-enter Mecca in 630 CE.

see also...

Islam

Methodist Church

Methodism is a Christian Protestant movement which grew out of the Church of England. It was founded by John Wesley who was an Anglican priest, born in 1703 CE. Other people who were very influential in the early days of Methodism include John Wesley's brother Charles, and an Anglican priest, George Whitfield. Methodism concurs with the main beliefs of the Protestant churches, but is characterised by perhaps less of a concern with the finer points of theology and a style of simplicity and straightforwardness in worship and the conduct of the church. Women are ordained as priests in the Methodist Church. Methodism has a well-deserved reputation for working to help those who are underprivileged in society, and for striving for more social equality. Perhaps the essence of Methodism is that the spiritual goal of the individual lies in achieving a personal devotion to, and understanding with, God.

John Wesley was very much committed to the principle of education for all, particularly for those sectors of society who in the eighteenth century would have had little access to education. He arranged to publish a variety of educational books for sale at an inexpensive price, and also established Methodist reading rooms.

As a complement to his educational activities he was also one of the early supporters of the idea of Sunday Schools. He held Methodist meetings in the open air and also adopted the notion of groups of Methodists meeting informally to develop a collective spirit as a religious community. John Wesley developed the initial structure of Methodism which was different from that of the Anglican Church. Methodists were organised into 'societies' which themselves were subsumed under 'circuits', each with a Methodist minister responsible. Methodism also used lay preachers, and encouraged ministers to change circuits from time to time.

see also...

Christianity

Moksha

In the classical Hindu tradition, moksha means release from the notion of the endless cycle of birth and death which is the normal destiny of the soul of human beings. Moksha can thus be seen as the salvation of the soul, or as release from the cycle of transmigration. Classical Hinduism proposes various methods by which the individual may attain moksha. The cycle of rebirth is known as *samsara*, and it is very much affected by the law of karma. This proposes that the human condition in which we find ourselves is the result of the good and bad deeds which we have performed in previous existences. Similarly, in our next existence, the condition of our life (which may include such aspects as social class and occupation) will be affected directly by our actions in our present existence.

For a Hindu this eternal dependence upon the law of karma is essentially undesirable. What is desired is a course of action or spiritual way of life which will assure an escape from the cycle of *samsara* and hence the soul will merge with God. One of the best known systems proposed for achieving salvation is yoga. This may be regarded as a component of the other principal schools of Hindu thought, or as a distinct system of practices of its own. Yoga generally involves a complex of practices such as body postures, breathing exercises, and meditation. Such techniques are often used as an end in themselves, but are also part of the classical techniques to attain salvation.

Another system for gaining moksha and one which has become well known in the West, is *vedanta*. This term means literally 'the end of the *Vedas*', and the main texts of *vedanta* are the *Upanishads*. Vedantists argue that the ultimate reality is Brahman, and that people may attain salvation or union with Brahman by means of meditational practices.

see also...

Hinduism; Karma; Mantra; Salvation; Upanishads

Mormon Church

The Mormon Church or, to use its fuller name, The Church of Jesus Christ of Latter-day Saints, is an American religious movement. It was established in 1830 by Joseph Smith who lived in Vermont. As a young man, Smith was somewhat uncertain as to which church he should join, and then it is claimed he was the subject of a vision of two heavenly people who suggested he should prepare to establish his own church. Later visions told him of religious texts inscribed on golden plates buried in a hillside near where he lived. Joseph Smith located the plates and, it is suggested, translated the texts, and published their contents as *The Book of Mormon* in 1830. This book claims that Jesus Christ visited America, and that the indigenous Americans are, in fact, descended from the lost tribes of Israel. The Mormons eventually settled in Illinois, but Joseph Smith was murdered in 1844. In his place, Brigham Young became the leader of the religious community.

The community was subject to a certain degree of criticism and harassment, and hence Brigham Young decided to set out with his followers to the Great Salt Lake in what was later to be the state of Utah. This was a long journey of great privation, but Brigham Young proved to be an inspirational leader.

The community arrived at the Salt Lake in 1847, and succeeded in establishing Salt Lake City. Mormons accept that the *Old Testament* and the *New Testament* do reveal the will of God, yet argue that they are inadequate of themselves and that the *Book of Mormon* is also needed as a scriptural text. In the early years of the development of the Mormon faith, polygamy was regarded as an acceptable practice. This resulted in considerable criticism for Mormons, and they eventually abandoned the custom in the late nineteenth century. Mormons are very strict in not consuming materials such as alcohol, tea and coffee, all of which they consider harmful to health.

see also...

Bible; Christianity

Mosque

The mosque fulfils a number of important functions for the Muslim community. It is a place of prayer, a community centre and also a place where Islamic teaching can take place. The classical design of a mosque usually incorporates two features. There is a dome which is symbolic of the universe, and a minaret which is used by the *muezzin* in the call to prayer.

The Muslim must undertake ritual washing before entering the mosque and should also remove shoes. The mosque has no furniture, simply an expanse of carpet. Muslims kneel down on their prayer mats and face towards Mecca for prayer. The principal prayer meeting is at noon on Fridays when the *imam* gives a sermon. In every mosque there is a niche in one wall (the *mihrab*) which indicates the direction of Mecca. Usually it is only men who attend the Friday noon prayers; but if women do so, they usually stand at the back of the prayer room. The mosque usually provides washing facilities for Muslims who are attending for prayer. In some countries these may be outside, but in colder climates are inside. Before washing, the Muslim says a prayer affirming that s/he is here to worship Allah in purity. Then follows the washing of the hands, the mouth and face, the arms, the head, ears and neck, and the feet.

In England, the Muslim community has created a great many mosques. Some are large and purpose built such as the Regent's Park Mosque in London, while others make use of a variety of converted buildings. The mosque is also an important centre when festivals are celebrated. An example is the festival of Eid-ul-Fitr which marks the end of the fasting period of Ramadan. The *imam* at the mosque marks the start of the festival by a sermon on the merits of giving to the poor. Islamic education is an important feature of life at the mosque, and there is often a school for Islamic study attached to the mosque.

see also...

Islam; Qur'an

Muhammad

Muhammad was the prophet believed by Muslims to have received a series of revelations from God, which were later collected together and called the *Qur'an*. Muhammad was thus the founder of Islam. He was born in Mecca in Arabia in about 570 CE, and died in Medina in 632 CE. At the time of Muhammad's birth Mecca was a thriving centre of commerce, largely built on trade with Mediterranean countries to the north. In Mecca was also located a religious shrine, the Kaaba, which attracted pilgrims from many parts of Arabia. Muhammad's early childhood was not easy. His father died before he was born, and his mother while he was still young. When his mother died his uncle, Abu Talib, became his guardian, and he taught him about commerce and trade. Eventually Muhammad married a widow named Khadija, who had considerable financial assets.

Although his wealth and success at commerce brought Muhammad social status in Mecca, he remained a person who was attached to contemplation and meditation. From time to time he went to a cave outside Mecca where he contemplated the spiritual life. On one occasion he had a vision of an angel who revealed insights from God. Muhammad continued to receive these divine revelations, and gradually developed the belief that he was a prophet selected by God to act as a means of transmitting His message to humanity. Muhammad was so convinced of the truth of God's message, that he preached on the streets of Mecca, urging people to recognise the one true God, and to submit to His will.

Following threats in Mecca, Muhammad and his followers took sanctuary in Yathrib (later called Medina).The Hijra or migration to Medina, took place in 622 CE. This is used as the start of the Islamic calendar. In Medina Islam started to expand, and eventually Mecca surrendered. Muhammad made a pilgrimage to the Kaaba, and then returned to Medina.

see also...

Islam; Mecca; Mosque; Qu'ran; Ramadan

Mysticism

This is the practice whereby a spiritual adept seeks to gain a direct and immediate religious experience. This experience is typically claimed to be beyond description. In other words, it is said to be so intense and so personal that to try to convey it to others would be futile.

Nevertheless, mystics do write about the techniques which may be used to try to gain such experience. The goal of the mystic quest may be variously expressed as a state of union with God, a direct experience of God, or a sense of communion with an all-pervading spirit in the universe. In the last sense, mysticism may not necessarily (although this is arguable) be associated with a transcendent God.

There is a mystical tradition in many of the world's major religions. Although it is somewhat of a generalisation, the mystical quest is often associated with the ascetic way of life and of withdrawal from the world. It is also often claimed by mystics that the only way of understanding the techniques required is to have the advice of a personal teacher. Finally, mystical practice often involves forms of meditation, sometimes associated with the repetition of a holy word or phrase, or repeating the name of God. Variants of such practices are found in a number of different traditions.

In Sufism, which is the mystical element in Islam, for example, one of the practices is called *dhikr*, which means remembering or repeating. The Sufi repeats over and over one of the names of God. In Buddhism one of the main practices involves concentration on the breath, the steady inhaling and exhaling through the nostrils. The regular practice of this technique is said to steady the mind, and enable the aspirant to understand the reality of the world more clearly.

see also...

Asceticism; Buddhist meditation; Tantrism; Yoga

Nibbana

Nibbana is the state of mind which is the ultimate purpose of the Buddhist. It is commonly known as enlightenment. Perhaps the feelings which accompany nibbana are difficult to describe; but on one level it is not a difficult concept. The human being is normally inclined to make life as comfortable as possible. S/he enjoys listening to music; likes pleasant and interesting food; likes to be surrounded with the company of loved ones; likes to feel secure with sufficient money and a nice house; and enjoys having a job which brings satisfaction and esteem. Yet the Buddhist tries to acknowledge that all of these things are impermanent (*anicca*). We may be made redundant at work, and may have to exchange our house for a smaller one. Although we do not like to think about it, eventually we will become ill and die. Hence, the Buddhist argues, if we become too attached to the sensory world we will eventually suffer badly, because the things of that world are impermanent. The sensory world is thus characterised by unsatisfactoriness (*dukkha*) and leads to suffering.

The Buddhist attempts, by using various meditative techniques, to weaken the attachment to the sensory world. The Buddhist tries to become less concerned when things do not go quite right. S/he tries to develop a sense of non-attachment.

In particular, Buddhists are conscious that we can become very attached to trying to develop as happy a lifestyle as possible. Human beings tend to look into the future to plan events in such a way that they will become happier still. Buddhists try as far as possible to live in the present moment, neither to regret the past, nor to plan too much for the future. They try to accept each moment as it comes learning from it and yet not worrying if it is not perfect. The ability to live in nibbana is said among other things to bring feelings of peace and a feeling of equanimity towards the world.

see also...

Buddhism; Buddhist meditation; Four Noble Truths

Noble Eightfold Path

This is the strategy which should be followed if people wish to gain an understanding of the world from the Buddhist point of view. Siddhartha Gautama, after he was enlightened and became the Buddha, outlined the Noble Eightfold Path in his first sermon in the deer park near Benares. This path constitutes the fourth of the Four Noble Truths, and provides an approach to life by which the individual may avoid the suffering which Buddhists feel arises from an attachment to worldly matters.

In brief, the Noble Eightfold Path consists of right understanding, right purpose, right speech, right conduct, right livelihood, right effort, right awareness, and right meditation. In more detail, right understanding involves the individual appreciating that there is no distinct human soul or self, and also that every aspect of the material world is subject to change. Right purpose involves the general decision to be kind to others and not to damage other living things. Right speech means being careful about what we say, not just by avoiding swearing or lying, but by avoiding talking about other people in an unpleasant way. Right conduct is an injunction not to kill other living things, not to be involved in any kind of theft, or for example, to drink alcohol to excess. Right livelihood is the recommendation that the Buddhist earns his or her living through a process which does not involve harming other living things. Hunting or fishing, for example, would normally be excluded as occupations. Right effort involves the strategy of not attaching to the 'pleasant' or 'unpleasant' features of the world around us. Right awareness is an encouragement for human beings to be completely aware of their own body, and of its mental and physical states. Finally, right meditation is designed to calm the mind and then to help the individual analyse the nature of existence.

see also...

Buddhism; Nibbana; Pali canon; Siddhartha Gautama

Non-violence

This is the philosophy that one should not do any harm to living things. It has a particularly long history in the Indian subcontinent and is often known by the Sanskrit word *ahimsa*.

Non-violence was already spreading throughout India in the third century BCE, but it received official support when the King of India, Asoka, who was crowned in 269 BCE, became a Buddhist. Asoka, prior to his conversion, had been an active military leader, but in a number of ways he changed when he became a Buddhist. In terms of military activity, he reduced this considerably, only using force when it was absolutely necessary to restrict incursions and aggressive activity by other rulers. He did not engage in the hunting of deer and other animals, and both he and his courtiers were largely vegetarian.

Buddhists have always tended to emphasise non-violence in their way of life. They have typically been vegetarian and in the approach of mindfulness have emphasised the need to be very careful in their day-to-day living, that they do no harm to other living creatures. Jainism has emphasised non-violence probably more than Buddhism. Jain monks typically filter drinking water to make sure they do not ingest living organisms, and also wear a gauze face mask to avoid breathing in organisms living in the air. Finally, they often carry a small brush with which to sweep the pathway ahead of themselves as they walk, so that they do not risk treading on a small organism.

Although *ahimsa* has been a factor in Hindu teaching, it was perhaps Mahatma Gandhi who raised it to a level where it became well known outside India. Gandhi employed the concept in the sense of cultivating a calm and friendly disposition towards people, but also advocated it as an approach in the political arena.

see also...

Buddhism; Hinduism; Jainism; Mahavira

Orthodox Church

There have, for about half the history of Christianity, been theological differences between what may be called the 'eastern' and 'western' Christian churches. In 330 CE Emperor Constantine founded Constantinople (the modern Istanbul) as the focus of the Christian Church in the east. The Bishop of Constantinople became the senior Patriarch of the eastern church, as issues of doctrine began to divide the church. There was a theological difference concerning the wording of the Creed, and this was not fully resolved. Finally, in 1054 CE, there was a point reached where the two branches of the church began to operate separately.

The word orthodox signifies 'correct belief'. Most of the churches within the framework of the Eastern Orthodox Church are located in Russia, Romania, Georgia and Greece. There is also a smaller group of churches located in Syria and Ethiopia. The Orthodox Church has a strong sense of religious ritual. The holy communion or eucharist is one of the main elements in worship within the Orthodox Church. The church building within the Orthodox Church is often shaped in the form of a cross. One of the characteristic features of Orthodox churches are the icons which decorate the walls. These are paintings of Christian figures such as Jesus, or the saints and apostles, often carried out on wooden blocks and surrounded by gold paintwork. The purpose of the icons is to bring the concept of the transcendent God within reach of worshippers, where they can worship God as an imminent figure.

A characteristic feature of an Orthodox Church is the iconostasis. This is a large screen decorated with icons, which separates the altar from the people in the congregation. In the centre of the iconostasis are two doors through which the priest comes for the celebration of eucharist.

see also...

Christianity; Church; Holy Communion; Prayer

Pali canon

These are the authorised scriptures of the Theravada School of Buddhism, which are written in the Pali language. The Buddha probably spoke in the Magadhi language, whereas when the teachings of the Buddha were finally written down, Pali was used.

When the Buddha died, his teachings were memorised by the monks and nuns, and passed on from generation to generation through techniques such as recitation. There was obviously a danger with this process that key teachings could be inadvertently altered or amended as the Buddha's sermons were transmitted. The accuracy of the transmission was very important, because the Buddha had emphasised that it was not he as a person who was important, but rather his teachings and the message contained therein.

In order to review the teachings and to resolve any uncertainties about what should or should not be included in the authorised scriptures, three major conferences were held. These are usually referred to as the First, Second and Third Buddhist Councils. The First Council was held at Rajagaha in 483 BCE, a few months after the death of the Buddha. It is a reasonable assumption that monks were still deeply affected by this event, and wished to meet to agree the key aspects of his teaching which were to be passed on. In about 383 BCE the Second Council met, again to check the teachings and ensure, as far as possible, accurate transmission. The monks and nuns looked particularly for any apparent disagreements in the teachings, and tried to eliminate inconsistencies. In 253 BCE the Third Council was held at Pataliputta, the present-day Patna. At this council it is suggested that up to 1,000 monks recited the scriptures. Eventually, in about 80 BCE, the Buddhist scriptures were transferred into written form to become the Pali canon.

see also...

Buddhism; Buddhist meditation; Siddhartha Gautama

Parsis

The Parsis are a religious minority living largely in the Bombay area of India. They were originally a migrant group of Zoroastrians from Persia, and, indeed, the word Parsi comes from the same root as Persia.

In the tenth century CE there was a degree of persecution of the Zoroastrians in Persia, and a group decided to leave, finally settling in the Bombay area in 936 CE. They were hospitably received by the local Hindus, and given a land grant upon which to start a new life. The industrial and commercial development of the Bombay hinterland under the British Raj enabled the Parsis to take advantage of their educational traditions, and to become economically powerful. They remain to this day a largely wealthy and influential minority.

Parsis have become westernised in some aspects of their secular lives and this influence has interacted with the practice of their religion. Nevertheless the essentials of the Zoroastrian tradition have been maintained. One of the most characteristic and well known features of Parsi culture is the method used to dispose of the dead. Parsis regard burial as a process which pollutes the earth and water and is hence undesirable. Fire is regarded as sacred, and so cremation is equally undesirable. Shortly after death is confirmed, the body is taken to a round, windowless building where it is laid on the roof. Clothing is removed from the body, and it is left. It does not take long for vultures to consume the body, leaving only the bones. Parsis regard this method of disposal as clean and natural.

Fire temples are a second important feature of Parsi religious life. The sacred fire is maintained by the priest, and the devotee comes to the temple usually alone, rather than in a group. The devotee prays to God while focusing upon the sacred fire. A symbolic piece of wood may be left for the priest to put on the fire.

see also...

Zoroastrianism

Passover

This is the event from the *Book of Exodus* in the *Old Testament* when God caused every first-born Egyptian child to die, yet spared ('passed over') the houses of the Israelites. Jews celebrate the fact that their first-born children were spared and that they managed to leave Egypt at the festival of *Pesach* or Passover. When Moses returned to Egypt, the Pharaoh was unwilling to release the Israelites from slavery, in which they had been held for over 400 years.

In order to punish the Egyptians, God sent a series of ten plagues, the final one being that all the first-born of the Egyptians should die. God, however, warned Moses that he should take steps to prevent the same happening to the first-born of the Israelites. Each family should kill a lamb and smear the blood on the door frame. Then during the night, when the Egyptians died, the Israelite families would be spared. The Israelites did what Moses asked, and in the morning the Pharaoh was aghast at what had happened. He finally released the Israelites after 430 years of slavery, and commanded them to leave immediately. The Israelites left in great haste, not even having time to leaven their bread. The contemporary festival of Pesach remembers these events, and on the eve of the Passover a meal is eaten which includes several symbolic representations of the rapid flight from Egypt after the plagues instituted by God. All leavened bread is removed from Jewish homes prior to the meal. Unleavened bread is eaten to remind people of the hasty departure from Egypt. Bitter herbs are eaten to remind Jews of the long period of slavery, and salty vegetables are eaten to recall the tears of the many years of forced labour in Egypt.

The escape from Egypt made an enormous impact on Jews, and today the significance of Passover is explained to younger people so that they will appreciate it as a celebration of freedom from slavery.

see also...

Judaism

Pilgrimage

A pilgrimage is a journey to a place of special spiritual significance. It need not necessarily involve a very long journey, and the individual may undertake a pilgrimage for a variety of reasons. It may be that within their particular faith it is regarded as a strongly desirable expression of devotion to God. Thus it might be felt to be a normative feature of religious behaviour. Contrariwise a pilgrimage may be considered by the individual to be a form of spiritual adventure, in order to try to discover something of the inner religious being. Alternatively, the person may hope to gain something from the devotional acts on the pilgrimage, for example the cure of an illness, or simply a sense of well-being and religious inspiration.

Buddhists tend to make pilgrimages, if possible, to the locations of the four principal events in the life of the historical Buddha. These are: the place of the birth of Siddhartha Gautama (Kapilavastu); the place where Siddhartha became enlightened (Bodh Gaya); the place where the Buddha preached his first sermon (Benares); and the place where the Buddha died (Kusinara). The perception which an individual Buddhist may have of a visit to these sites may depend somewhat on the particular school of Buddhism to which s/he belongs. The pilgrimage may be supposed to bring religious merit, or more generally to be inspirational and to encourage a reaffirmation of religious practice.

For Muslims the Hajj or pilgrimage to Mecca, is one of the Five Pillars of Islam, and is expected to be carried out by every devout Muslim, provided that s/he is sufficiently healthy and can manage to pay for the journey. The Hajj is a matter of great significance for Muslims, and among other things is symbolic of the equality of all Muslims.

There are many Christian places of pilgrimage. One of the most famous in England is to Canterbury Cathedral where Thomas à Beckett was murdered in 1170 CE.

---

see also...

Benares; Buddhism; Hajj; Mecca; Siddhartha Gautama

Prayer

The act of communicating with God is an important feature of many religions, although almost by definition it is a feature only of theistic religions. In Christian churches there is considerable variety in both the form and location of prayer. Prayer may be individualistic and private, or it may take place in a church, as part of a collective service and led by the priest. The wording of prayers may be established as in the Lord's Prayer, part of a formally agreed prayer book, or may be developed by the individual. The act of prayer has a number of specific functions including the asking of God for forgiveness, and the asking of God to help others – known as prayers of intercession. Contemplation and meditation are religious activities related to prayer, but do not imply the same employment of words in a dialogue with God. Some Christians use aids in prayer such as the rosary in the Roman Catholic Church. The beads in the rosary are used as a means of focusing the mind on the appropriate prayer to be said. Forms of prayer beads are also used in other traditions such as Hinduism.

In Islam, one of the most important duties of a Muslim is regular prayer. Muslims may pray as individuals in private prayer, but they are expected to take part in the ritual prayer which is normally carried out five times each day. The times of prayer are usually at dawn, midday, mid-afternoon, evening and night. Prayers may be said at the mosque, or elsewhere using a prayer mat to create an appropriate place. Ritual prayers are known as *salah*. All male Muslims are expected to attend the noon prayers on Fridays at the mosque, when the *imam* gives a sermon. When praying a Muslim should face in the direction of Mecca.

In Judaism, prayer is also a very important activity. Many of the prayers are well established and contained in the prayer book. The best known prayer of all is the *shema*. At morning prayer Jews traditionally wear phylacteries on the head, which are small boxes containing extracts from the scriptures.

see also...

Christianity; Islam; Judaism

Quakers

The Quakers, otherwise known as the Society of Friends, constitute a non-conformist Protestant movement which developed in England in the mid-seventeenth century. The founder of the Quaker movement was George Fox, and he appears to have been motivated by a desire for direct contact with God, and comprehension of Him. There was an assumption that there was no need for a specially trained person such as a priest to intercede between the individual and God. Similarly in the Quaker tradition, there is no special use of ceremonial, or of prayer or hymn books. A Quaker gathering usually involves members sitting in an approximate circle for a period of quiet contemplation. If, at some point in the contemplation, members feel the need to share a spiritual thought with others, they may articulate their thoughts. Quakers have interpreted their faith very much in terms of the need to help with areas of social concern.

In addition to spreading across England, the Quakers became established in North America, notably in the state of Pennsylvania, named after the Quaker, William Penn. During their early history, the Quakers suffered considerable persecution, and in fact were prohibited from certain occupations such as an academic profession or a career in the civil service. One possible consequence of this is that Quakers frequently excelled in other areas, such as business and commerce. Quakers were also very cautious in financial matters, and established a considerable reputation for fairness in matters of trade and finance. Business people were thus very confident when dealing with Quakers, and many Quakers became very wealthy. Typically such wealth was used to establish educational foundations, or to help with needy social causes.

Quakers were at the forefront of the reform of the prison system, and of the campaigns for the abolition of slavery and capital punishment.

see also...

Christianity

Qur'an

The *Qur'an* is the holy book of Islam, and constitutes a collection of the revelations made to the prophet Muhammad by God. In the view of Muslims the original of the *Qur'an* exists in heaven, and it was gradually revealed to Muhammad. As it is regarded as God's revelation the *Qur'an* is treated with great respect. Copies of it are usually kept wrapped in rich material. A copy of the *Qur'an* is usually placed in a specially reserved position, well apart from other books. So significant is the Qur'an that devout Muslims will often attempt to learn it from beginning to end, and recite it from memory. Indeed the word *Qur'an* comes from an Arabic word meaning 'to recite', and hence the *Qur'an* is a book designed for recitation.

While Muhammad was still living, the individual revelations from God were either memorised for oral transmission, or they were written on convenient materials like dried palm leaves, and flat stones or bones. After his death there was an understandable urge to consolidate the content of the *Qur'an*, and to establish an agreed and standard book. At this time probably the most common method of remembering the *Qur'an* was by means of regular repetitive recitation. There have been disagreements about how the composition of the *Qur'an* was finally established. Certainly work proceeded during the first two years after Muhammad's death, when Abu Bakr led the Muslim community, and also the next ten years of the Caliph Umar's leadership. It seems likely that the agreed version of the *Qur'an* was established during the 12 years from 644 CE onwards, while Uthman was the Caliph. The chapters of the *Qur'an* are called *suras*. The longer *suras* tend to be placed near the beginning of the *Qur'an*. Each *sura* is normally named after a word or term which occurs quite near the beginning of each *sura*, for example, 'Angels' or 'The Fig'. Muslims regard the *Qur'an* as the complete revelation of God.

see also...

Islam; Muhammad

Ramadan

Ramadan is the ninth month of the Islamic calendar. Its particular significance is that the fourth of the Five Pillars of Islam places a duty on Muslims to go without food and drink between sunrise and sunset throughout the entirety of the month of Ramadan. A particularly important aspect of Ramadan is that on the 27th day of the month, the prophet Muhammad received the first of the revelations from God which are enshrined in the *Qur'an*. The night of the 27th day of the month is hence known as the Night of Power. When Ramadan occurs during the hotter times of the year, it requires considerable discipline to sustain the fast. One of the benefits of the fast is that it acts as a reminder to Muslims of the kind of privations which are suffered by people in poorer parts of the world.

For Muslims the fasting process helps them to focus their minds on God, and on the physical benefits which He brings to mankind. Some categories of people are exempt from fasting during Ramadan. These include people who are ill, or the elderly. Pregnant women or those travelling on long journeys also need not participate. Children are gradually introduced to the purposes and customs of fasting as they get older.

The pattern of the day during Ramadan is that people rise from bed very early in order to have a meal before sunrise. The fast then commences for the duration of the day. Once sunset has arrived people can break the fast with a small meal, followed by a larger meal later in the evening. Muslims will often visit the mosque for prayers during the evenings of Ramadan, and many read the whole *Qur'an* during the month, reading a part each evening. The end of Ramadan is signified by the festival of Id-ul-Fitr which is a three-day festival. People exchange presents and Id cards, and families gather together to have special celebratory meals.

see also...

Islam; Muhammad

Rastafarianism

astafarianism is a religious movement which originated in Jamaica, and which looks to Haile Selassie, the former Emperor of Ethiopia, as having been a messiah for black people everywhere. Rastafarians tend to view Ethiopia, and more generally Africa, as a kind of homeland, to which they will eventually return. Rastafarians possess a mixture of beliefs. There is a close relationship with the history of Judaism and Christianity, and with the theology of the *Old Testament*. They believe that their stay in Jamaica has been essentially a punishment for past sinful behaviour, and, this having been redeemed, they should now move back to Africa. Rastafarians believe that black people are essentially superior to white people, although this does not indicate that they reject white people. In fact, there are a number of white members of the Rastafarian movement. At their meetings Rastafarians pray and conduct readings from the *Bible*.

There is a broad set of agreements on the way Rastafarians should behave. They generally reject the value systems of a white, materialistic, westernised society. They are largely vegetarian in eating, and they avoid cutting the hair, shaving or decorating the skin as in tattooing. The *Bible* is regarded with great reverence by the Rastafarians, although not all sections of it are equally esteemed. They believe that in the translation process from the original language, an ideology which supported white supremacist views became evident.

Rastafarians are well known for using marijuana or *ganga*. It is used in religious ceremonies to aid meditational practice, and for recreation. In some ways *ganga* is used as a symbol of opposition to white, mainstream society. Although Rastafarians smoke *ganga*, they are generally opposed to the drinking of spirits, and to the smoking of normal cigarettes. One of the characteristic symbols of the Rastafarians is the wearing of long hair, or 'dreadlocks'.

see also...

Christianity; Judaism

Rebirth

ebirth is a Buddhist concept which is to be distinguished from reincarnation. The latter, in whatever spiritual tradition it is found, tends to assume that upon death, the soul or other entity of a living thing, passes to the body of a new organism. Similarly it is assumed that living things now may have received the souls of previous living things.

Rebirth, however, is a very different concept. To some extent it follows from the Buddhist notion of impermanence. The human body and mind, according to the idea of impermanence, are continually changing. In youth the body is growing, and the body cells are actively dividing. At a cellular level, the body changes throughout life, and changes at that level are ultimately reflected in external appearance. Similarly, the mind changes. Our attitudes to things do not remain constant. Fresh ideas come and go in our mind.

To broaden out the concept of impermanence, we may see the entire universe as being in a process of flux. On this view we tend to see a very long continuum of change with the birth and death of individual organisms simply being points on this continuum. Hence, death is not viewed in Buddhist terms as being the end of existence, but merely a stage in the continuous sequence of life and death, which is termed impermanence.

Rebirth is also linked to the concept of karma, or the doctrine of cause and effect. The principle of karma suggests that everything we say or do has a consequence for both ourselves and other people. Buddhists argue that rebirth is not a phenomenon to be proved, or a theory in which to believe. Rather, it is a process which people can see happening around them.

see also...

Buddhism; Impermanence; Karma; Nibbana

Resurrection

This term is used in the Christian faith to explain the disappearance of the body of Jesus from the tomb and Jesus' appearance to his disciples, after he had been executed by the Romans. The belief in the resurrection of Jesus Christ after his crucifixion is a central element of Christian faith. The accounts of the resurrection in the gospels differ slightly. In Matthew's gospel, for example, Joseph of Arimathaea managed to persuade Pilate to let him have the body of Jesus, which he then placed in a tomb of his own, and sealed with a heavy stone. After three days Mary Magdalene and another woman came to the tomb, but the stone had been rolled away from the entrance and an angel was sitting upon it. He said to the women that Jesus was risen and that he had gone to Galilee where he would meet his disciples. As the women were on their way to meet the disciples and give them the news of what they had observed, Jesus appeared to them. Later Jesus also appeared to the 11 disciples.

In Mark's gospel Pilate releases the body of Jesus to Joseph of Arimathaea once he has confirmed with the centurion that Jesus was actually dead. Mary Magdalene and two other women bring aromatic spices to anoint the body of Jesus. They are concerned about managing to roll away the heavy stone which seals the tomb. When they arrive they see that the stone has already been rolled away, and on entering the tomb they see a young man dressed in a long white robe. He tells the women that Jesus is risen. They should go and tell the disciples that Jesus will appear to them in Galilee. Subsequently, Jesus appeared to Mary Magdalene, to two of the disciples, and finally to the 11 disciples.

Looking at these events it is possible to suggest a number of explanations. However, Christians believe that the true explanation is that God raised Jesus from the dead.

see also...

Christianity; Jesus

Roman Catholic Church

The Roman Catholic Church is one of the three principal traditions of Christianity, the others being the Orthodox Church and the Protestant Church. The Church gradually grew within the Roman Empire with people being influenced by, among other factors, its ethical stance. When the Church grew to a significant size it caused some consternation with the Roman authorities and there were major persecutions under emperors such as Diocletian. During the third century CE there were gradual developments in the formal organisation and administration of the Church, and in the clarification of authorised scripture. By 314 CE, the Church was formally accepted as a religion and towards the end of the century became the religion of the Roman Empire.

Throughout the ensuing years the role of the Church became more and more entwined with secular society in Europe. From the end of the eleventh century onwards, there was a gradual increase in the authority of the Pope, which was supported by legal and theological arguments. The influence of Rome was not accepted everywhere, however, and in the sixteenth century there was a general movement challenging the Roman Catholic Church. In 1517 Martin Luther challenged the authority of the Pope and what he saw as the dogma of the Church. This process ushered in the so-called Reformation. Other key influences were Zwingli and Calvin.

Some states separated from Rome and established their own Protestant or reformed churches. From the mid-sixteenth century onwards, however, the Catholic Church attempted to address some of the Protestant criticisms, and to institute reforms. This movement became known as the Counter-Reformation. In 1870 the doctrine of Papal Infallibility was promulgated, but throughout the twentieth century there was a gradual opening up of the Church to external influence.

see also...

Anglican Communion;
Christianity; Church

Sabbath

The Sabbath or Shabbat is the holy day in Judaism. It is considered as starting on Friday evening at sunset, lasting until sunset on Saturday evening. It is regarded as a commandment of God to keep the Sabbath. On the Friday evening, at the start of the Sabbath, candles are lit in the home. Traditionally, the father of the family says a special prayer called the *kiddush*, which asks for his family to be blessed. A service is held during the evening which marks the creation of heaven and earth by God. The Sabbath meal is then eaten, and as part of it there are plaited loaves. The dough is intertwined to act as a reminder of the relationship between the Jewish people, the *Torah* and God.

On the Saturday morning Jews attend the traditional Sabbath service at the synagogue. It has been part of Jewish tradition that men and women sit separately during the service. It is the norm for men to wear skull caps and a *tallith*, or prayer shawl. The service in an Orthodox synagogue will be in Hebrew, although in other synagogues it is possible for the service to be held in other languages. The service starts with prayers and psalms. The rabbi is the spiritual head of the synagogue, but usually does not lead the service. This is done by the *chazan* or reader, who takes a leading role in the singing.

The *Torah* is removed from the Ark and carried through the congregation, where people may touch it. Readings from the *Torah* then take place. Traditionally it is men who read, but in Reform synagogues, women may read. There may also be a sermon delivered by the rabbi, which discusses some elements of the reading from the *Torah*. The rest of the Sabbath day is spent quietly and finally there is a short ceremony which ends the Sabbath.

see also...

Covenant; Judaism; Passover; Synagogue; Torah

Sadhu

A sadhu is the term used for a religious ascetic in India. Sadhus vary widely in appearance and lifestyle, but in general terms they share some features. They are religiously motivated, either through devotion to a personal deity or through the general aim to use yogic or mystical practices to attain union with Brahman, the ultimate reality. Such union, they believe, will result in moksha or release from the cyclic nature of human reincarnation. To some extent all sadhus sever contact with mainstream society. They will typically have very few possessions, and may carry only an alms bowl or container for carrying water. They wear relatively limited clothing, usually of a saffron or ochre colour, the traditional colour for the monk or nun in India. Some sects of sadhus are entirely naked, perhaps covering themselves in ashes or smearing themselves in clay.

Many sadhus or *sannyasins* lead an itinerant life, wandering alone or in groups between holy places. Others may live simply outside a village or town where they receive alms from local inhabitants in exchange for spiritual and practical advice. Some may establish a small *ashram* which local people will come to visit. Laypeople may variously regard sadhus with affection and respect, and see them as people of God; some people, however, regard them as a nuisance – as people who take advantage of conventional society.

A sadhu may act as a guru or teacher to a younger person, who will act as a combination of student and servant. In turn the sadhu will himself or herself have a guru who taught them their particular religious tradition. Sadhus will generally practice yoga postures, meditate and pray, fast as appropriate, and occasionally engage in ascetic acts of various kinds. The scriptures contain accounts of the discipline of being a sadhu. In Chapter 6 of the *Bhagavad Gita*, Krishna explains how a *sannyasin* should behave and conduct himself.

see also...

Hinduism

Salvation

Salvation is the process whereby the spiritual element in a human being is lifted from the material plane into a different level of being associated either with God or with at least existence in a spiritual realm. Salvation includes the concept of transformation from the ordinary to the spiritual. There may be an implicit concept of eternity in a spiritual existence or of life everlasting. Salvation may also be considered as taking place during the life of an individual, or else only at death. In the former case there is an implicit sense of a radical change in lifestyle or belief system which enables the individual to be spiritually transformed. In the latter case there may be an assumption about the intervention of God or of the judgement of God, allowing the individual to live after death in a heavenly realm.

In Christianity it is believed that if individuals commit themselves to the teachings of Jesus and believe in Him, they will gain everlasting life and live in heaven with God forever. There is the belief that death is not the end of life, but for Christians the beginning of a new life. Buddhists, by the same token, have a rather different view. They place much more emphasis upon the quality of life in the here and now. Indeed, they do not normally concern themselves with the question of what happens after death. They prefer to concentrate fully on the way in which they conduct their existence in the present.

For Hindus, the whole of life is related to trying to achieve moksha or liberation from the cycle of rebirth. Various techniques may be used including yoga and meditation. The Hindu is also expected to carry out the functions and duties in life which are associated with him or her through their role in society. Ultimately, through a life of devotion and meditation, the individual will become merged with Brahman, and will gain salvation from the cycle of birth and death.

see also...

Buddhism; Christianity; Hinduism

Sangha

When the Buddha had achieved enlightenment he walked to the deer park at Sarnath near Benares, and outlined his ideas on spiritual liberation to five wandering mendicants whom he had known previously. They recognised the profundity of what he was saying, and became the first monks of the sangha, or community of monks. The sangha may be thought of as the ordained monks and nuns, or, in a broader sense, as all people who are trying to lead the disciplined and virtuous Buddhist life.

Whether in a monastery or leading the wandering homeless life, monks or nuns have few possessions. They dress in a simple ochre or brown robe and wear sandals. They carry an alms bowl in which laypeople may place simple food requirements. The monk or *bhikkhu* lives the simplest of lives, eating only sufficient to maintain the health of the body, and normally not handling money. The alms, provided by laypeople out of respect for the Buddha's teachings, are expected to be adequate to sustain life. The process of becoming a member of the ordained sangha is a formal matter. A novice is termed an *anagarika*, and must commit to leading a particular form of life. The *anagarika* is assumed to have renounced the everyday life of a householder, and to abide by the discipline of the ordained Buddhist. In particular he or she must abide by the so-called Eight Precepts. The *anagarika* is expected to follow the discipline for a year or two, before deciding whether to commit to full ordination.

Within a monastery context the ordained sangha will rise before dawn, and typically spend a period of time chanting from the scriptures and in meditation. The rest of the day may be devoted to work or teaching, followed by an evening period of meditation.

see also...

Buddhism; Buddhist meditation; Noble Eightfold Path

Sanskrit

Sanskrit is the classical Indian language in which the religious texts of India, such as the *Vedas* and *Upanishads*, were written. Part of the interest of Sanskrit in the West is that it appears to be related to many of the main European languages; Indian and European languages have evolved from the language spoken by the tribes of the southern Asian plains in about 2000 BCE.

Knowledge of Sanskrit in the West was first due to several English administrators who had an interest in Indian culture. Sir William Jones of the Supreme Court in Calcutta, and Charles Wilkins of the East India Company, mastered Sanskrit in the eighteenth century. The first Sanskrit work to be translated into English was the *Bhagavad Gita*, translated by Charles Wilkins. In the nineteenth century professorships of Sanskrit were established at the Collège de France in Paris, and at the University of Oxford, and from then on it became an established area of university study.

Sanskrit as a language was developing continuously until about the fourth century BCE when a linguist named Panini produced a highly systematic grammar of it. From that time onwards, there were relatively few changes to the language, as the priests and government administrators regarded Panini's grammar as the definitive statement on the structure of Sanskrit.

One of the characteristics of Sanskrit are the cerebral consonants. This type of pronunciation was probably borrowed by the Aryan invaders from the indigenous inhabitants of India. Sanskrit was for many years transmitted orally, but eventually the *devanagari* script was adopted for the language. This is the same script in which modern Hindi is written. Sanskrit has always been the language used principally by the priestly caste, and it was probably used relatively little outside this social stratum.

see also...

Hinduism

Scripture

Most religions have writings which are regarded as holy and which express, among other things, the fundamental tenets of the faith. Scriptures sometimes also contain historical material which documents some features of the development of the religion.

In a number of cases, scriptures were originally transmitted orally before having their contents finally agreed and being committed to writing. Examples of initial oral transmission include the *Vedas* in Hinduism, and the teachings and sermons of the Buddha. There are differences between religions in terms of the importance attached to scriptures. In the Sikh religion the *Guru Granth Sahib* is regarded with great reverence and occupies a central place in the gurdwara. In Islam, the *Qur'an* is of enormous significance as it is regarded as the revealed word of God. Great importance is also attached to the Arabic language in which the *Qur'an* was originally revealed. Many Muslims would not regard it as acceptable to translate the *Qur'an* into other languages. The content of the *Qur'an* is also regarded as fixed and unchangeable.

Sometimes scriptures are compilations of religious writings, and generally the names of the authors and of the compiler are known. This is the case, for example, with the *Guru Granth Sahib*.

Scriptural writings are used in a variety of ways by different faiths. In Theravada Buddhism for instance, there is a strong tradition of passing on meditation teaching from generation to generation through the monks and nuns of the sangha. Here there is perhaps less of a focus by laypeople upon reading and studying the texts which recorded (originally in Pali) the teachings of the Buddha. In Islam, however, there is much more of a focus upon a person studying the *Qur'an* and even learning to recite it by heart. There is a related although not identical emphasis upon reading and studying scriptures in Judaism and Christianity.

see also...

Buddhism; Hinduism; Islam; Torah

Sects

A religious sect is a group of people who follow a religious tradition which cannot at the time be regarded as part of the mainstream belief system of society. They are thus typically characterised by a heterodox set of beliefs and practices, yet these may not remain heterodox for ever.

Ultimately, the religious principles of a sect may gradually become orthodox as the sect expands in membership and popularity; its creeds become more widely accepted; and it is generally seen as not being too radical for society to accept. It is through such a gradual process of evolution and social acceptance that a sect may win acceptance as a mainstream tradition. It is almost inevitable that a religion that has been revealed or articulated by a single individual will start with only a few adherents. Alternatively, some sects will not win the general acceptance of society, either because they are far removed from the prevailing orthodoxy, or perhaps because of some features of the social organisation of the sect. For some of the reasons mentioned above it is difficult to define the characteristics of a sect precisely. In addition, although the term may have some pejorative connotations, it does not necessarily follow that a sect is in any way undesirable, in either a religious or social sense. All that one can do is to map out something of the conceptual territory of the term.

In a general sense, then, sects are often associated with a single leader who exercises considerable, if not absolute, control over the collective life of members. To some extent this may be because the sect members in effect submit to such leadership.

Alternatively, one may argue that it is a feature of some sects that there is an element of psychological control over the sect members. A feature of some sects is that there appears to be limited autonomy in relation to religious matters.

Shi'a

The Shi'a are one of the two main divisions of Islam, but are not as numerous as the Sunni. These two divisions came into being because of differences of opinion about who should succeed Muhammad as leader of the Muslim community. When Muhammad died he was succeeded in turn by three caliphs, Abu Bakr, Umar and then Uthman. There was a group of Muslims who all along had considered that Ali, the son-in-law of Muhammad, should have succeeded him, and certainly should have become the caliph after Uthman. This group was the beginning of the Shi'a. During the conflict over who was going to be caliph, Ali was assassinated. Later, in 680 CE, Husayn, who was Ali's son, was killed. The Shi'a believe that the correct leader of all Muslims should be someone who is descended from the marriage of Ali and Fatima, who was the daughter of Muhammad. Such a leader is known to the Shi'a as the *imam*.

Within Shi'a there are three principal groupings, depending exactly on who one considers should have been in the succession of *imams* after Ali.

One group believes that the fifth *imam* should have been Muhammad al-Baqir, the grandson of Husayn, while another believes that Zayd, the brother of al-Baqir should have been the *imam*. The supporters of al-Baqir themselves split later over the issue of who should be the seventh *imam*. The Ismailis considered that Ismail should be the *imam*, while others supported Ismail's younger brother, Musa. The followers of Musa consider that there were 12 *imams*, and that the 12th *imam* disappeared. This group feels that there is always an *imam* on earth to provide guidance from God. A comprehensive system of clerics has developed to provide guidance on religious matters.

The followers of Zayd also have the concept of *imam*, but feel that anyone in principle can be *imam* as long as they are descended from either Husayn or his brother Hasan. The Ismailis eventually established the well-known university of Al-Azhar in Cairo.

see also...

Islam; Sunnis

Shinto

Shinto is the original religion of Japan. It is not possible to give a precise date as to when the religion began, or to name one single specific founder. In the nineteenth century CE Shinto became the official religion of Japan, but it declined in importance after the Second World War. An important aspect of Shinto is a belief in *kamis*, which may be conceived as nature spirits or gods. There are many different *kamis* which are worshipped, but perhaps the most significant is Amaterasu, the Sun Goddess.

Religious shrines are also of great importance in Shinto. There are many different shrines, some of simply local importance and others of great national significance. Shrines often have some architectural features in common. The shrine is often built in a peaceful, natural setting. The central aspect of the shrine is the *honden*, which is a small building in which there is a symbolic representation of the deity of the shrine. The *honden* tends to be used only by the priest of the shrine. However, there is usually also a larger room, the *haiden*, which is used by groups of visitors to the shrine for prayer or other forms of worship.

Shrines are established for many kinds of reasons. They may be devoted to a local natural feature such as a river, or to a significant historical person. The entrance to a shrine is often marked by a large gate with a very characteristic design. These gates are known as *torii*. They are typically composed of two heavy upright wooden pillars, and two cross-pieces, the uppermost of which often curves upwards at the ends. When an individual visits a shrine, s/he will ring a bell and clap hands at the entrance. The purpose of this is to let the deity know that a devotee is present. The visitor will also make a small monetary donation to the shrine. After saying prayers, the person will again sound a bell, clap hands and depart.

see also...

Zen

Shiva

Shiva is one of the great gods of Hinduism. He is often associated with destruction, but there are many aspects to the personality of Shiva including those of the religious ascetic and of the creator of life.

Shiva is perhaps best known as a statue representing the Lord of the Dance (Nataraja). Tamil bronzes are well-known examples of such images. Shiva is shown dancing within a circle of flames which represents the universe. He has four arms, and stands with one foot on a demon. In the palm of one hand is a flame representing the destruction and creation of the universe, and in another hand is a small drum with which he beats the rhythm of the universe. Snakes, over which he has power, writhe around his neck.

The presence of opposites in one deity is shown, on the one hand, by Shiva being associated with places of death, such as sites of cremation. He is supposed to wear a necklace of skulls, and to be accompanied by spirits. On the other hand, he is associated as described above with dancing, and also as a meditative

ascetic. He is often conceptualised as the great yogi, meditating on the universe. He is symbolised as wearing a crescent moon in his hair, and holding a trident. He is covered in ashes, a practice which is very common among sadhus. Shiva is usually pictured as having a third eye in the centre of his forehead, which is associated with his additional understanding of the universe.

In many temples Shiva is worshipped as a stone symbol of the phallus, usually called a *lingam*. In this form Shiva represents fertility and hence the creation of the universe. He is also sometimes portrayed as a teacher or form of guru. Shiva is married to Parvati, and he is also often portrayed accompanied by a white bull, Nandi.

see also...

Hinduism; Karma; Krishna; Moksha; Vishnu

Siddhartha Gautama

Siddhartha Gautama is the original family name of the young man who became known, on his spiritual enlightenment, as the Buddha. He established the Buddhist religion and founded the sangha or community of Buddhist monks and nuns.

He was born around 563 BCE, the son of King Suddhodhana, the leader of the Sakya people of what is now southern Nepal. After his birth, according to tradition, it was predicted that he would become either a great worldly leader, or a great wandering spiritual teacher. His father was somewhat concerned that his son might become a religious ascetic, and presumably preferred that he would succeed him in ruling the kingdom. To this end, he attempted to ensure that Siddhartha led a very comfortable life within the palace, surrounded by every worldly pleasure that the king could provide. However, ever curious about the outside world, Siddhartha travelled beyond the palace grounds and witnessed an elderly man, a man suffering from disease and a dead man. On enquiring of his companion, Channa, he was told that this was the destiny of all human life. He finally saw a sadhu, or mendicant, and realised that some people devoted their lives to trying to understand the nature of existence.

Eventually he determined that he would have to leave his family, and himself become a wandering ascetic. Finally he sat to meditate under a tree near the town of Gaya. During this meditation he came to an understanding of both the meaning of existence and of the process whereby others could gain his experience. He became the Buddha – or one who is enlightened. For approximately 40 years the Buddha outlined his philosophy to people in northern India. He died at the age of approximately 80, near the town of Kusinara.

---

see also...

Buddhism; Buddhist meditation; Noble Eightfold Path

Sikhism

ikhism is one of the principal faiths of India, although as Sikhs have migrated to many different parts of the world, the Sikh faith and culture have become known in other countries. Sikhism was founded by Guru Nanak, who was born in 1469 in Panjab in northern India. Nanak received a good education, but fairly early in his life showed an inclination for the religious, contemplative life. As a young man he left his family and embarked on a series of journeys during which he engaged in discussions with other religious people, preached, and meditated on the true nature of the religious life. Guru Nanak lived at a time of considerable conflict between Hindus and Muslims, and he was a strong advocate of peaceful coexistence between the two faiths. A very common tradition at the time, as indeed it still is today, was for some Hindus to withdraw from the world and lead the life of ascetics or sadhus. Guru Nanak suggested that this was not the most appropriate approach to the spiritual life and advocated people living within the confines of family life, yet devoting their lives to God. Part of the purpose of this suggestion was that by living in the world, rather than excluded from it, people could try to counteract the unfairness of social and political life.

Hinduism was, at the time, a religion firmly embedded in a system of social stratification, reflecting the caste system. Guru Nanak saw the inequality and unfairness of such a system, and preached the concept of the equality of all people. He particularly noticed the extent to which religious ritual was important in different faiths, and argued that people should really focus upon the nature of God and on the process of attaining union with God. Although there is an individualistic element here, in terms of the human being obtaining an understanding of God, nevertheless, there is a strong moral element, in terms of the duty of the individual to help the rest of humanity.

see also...

Guru Nanak

Sri Aurobindo

Aurobindo Ghose (1872–1950) usually known as Sri Aurobindo, was an Indian religious philosopher and writer, and also a political activist, who studied at the University of Cambridge. He subsequently held university posts in India, and became a student of the Indian religious tradition. In 1908 he was imprisoned by the British authorities in India, for actively supporting the independence of India. He later moved to Pondicherry in southern India, and there established a world famous centre for spiritual studies.

Aurobindo was a student of the *Bhagavad Gita* and wrote an analysis of his views on the *Gita*'s philosophy. He argued that in order for human beings to have a spiritual, rather than a worldly oriented consciousness they had to try to achieve union with God and to dedicate all their actions to God. Aurobindo considered that on one level there was a single unified spiritual power in the universe, but that individual human beings were manifestations of that spiritual power. It was one of the main functions of yoga to enable each individual to realise his/her relationship to every other human being and to the spiritual absolute of the universe.

Aurobindo tends to advocate a compromise between the materialist philosophies of the West, and the more extreme religious asceticism of some aspects of Hinduism. He considers that the most appropriate route for spiritual evolution is a combination of the material and the spiritual. Aurobindo was keen to state that he did not see himself as any particular type or status of religious guru, but rather that he wished to help others in their spiritual journey. He did not wish to create a new religious movement or type of yoga, but to encourage human beings to see something of the spiritual universe, and incorporate it into their daily lives.

see also...

Asceticism; Bhagavad Gita; Hinduism; Yoga

Sufism

Sufism is the mystical tradition in Islam which developed early in the history of the faith. Sufis developed a way of life which was very simple, and in many ways involved relinquishing the material things of the world. The purpose of Sufis was to attain a direct comprehension of God.

The word Sufi may have derived from the Arabic word for wool (*suf*) reflecting the practice of wearing woollen garments. Sufis developed a variety of practices in order to try to attain a direct experience of God. Among the variety of practices are long periods of prayer and meditation, often in a solitary situation, and in a quiet, peaceful location. Many Sufis either live in, or are part of, a monastic community.

One of the long-standing traditions of Sufism is that the aspirant should receive instruction from an experienced Sufi teacher. The Sufi also tries to discard many of the material accompaniments of society. The reason for this is that it is assumed that material possessions and desires are an obstacle to spiritual progress, since they tend to remove the attention of the individual from God. A particular spiritual technique used by Sufis is termed *dhikr*, which means remembering or repeating. It signifies the practice of repeating the name of God over and over again. This technique is aimed at calming the mind, helping the mind to exclude non-religious thoughts, and to help the individual to focus upon God. The condition of achieving a direct experience of God is very difficult to describe, yet it is sometimes conceptualised as involving the merging of the soul of the individual with the soul of God. The word *fana* which means extinction, is used to describe this process. Extinction here refers to the merging of the human soul in the divine soul. When a group of disciples gathered around an accepted Sufi teacher, they would eventually take on students themselves. In this way Sufi teachings would be passed on from generation to generation.

see also...

Islam

Sunnis

The Sunnis are the majority grouping within Muslim society constituting about 90 per cent of all Muslims. The other grouping is known as the Shi'a. The differences between the two groups date back to the issues surrounding the leadership of the Muslim community after the death of Muhammad. As Muslims believed that the *Qur'an* was the final and complete work of God, and that this had been revealed to the prophet Muhammad, the Sunnis argued that the only appropriate role for a leader of the community would be a 'caliph' or representative. Such a person would act as an administrator of the community, and would live and act in accordance with the principles of the *Qur'an*. The caliphs after Muhammad's death were Abu Bakr (632–634 CE); Umar (634–644 CE); and Uthman (644–656 CE).

When Uthman died there followed a period of conflict and dispute over who should succeed him as caliph. Some felt that Ali who was the prophet Muhammad's son-in-law should be caliph, while others supported Mu'awiya who was a cousin of Uthman. Ali was eventually assassinated, and Mu'awiya took control of the community. The Shi'a felt that Ali should have been the leader of the Muslim community.

From the beginning the Sunnis feel they have acted for the benefit of the Muslim community as a whole. They would argue that, following Muhammad's death, Abu Bakr did not particularly seek to be appointed caliph, and only did so because he felt he could bring some sense of unity to the Muslim community. Much the same type of argument is used to support the appointments of Umar and Uthman. Sunnis are generally willing to accept that Ali had a reasonable claim to the leadership, but feel that the most appropriate people were probably selected. The Shi'a do not accept this, and consider that there is a tradition which suggests that Muhammad himself wished Ali to succeed him.

see also...

Islam; Muhammad; Shi'a

Synagogue

The synagogue is the place where Jews gather for a variety of purposes including prayer. It should be remembered, however, that a great deal of Jewish devotion traditionally takes place in the home. The synagogue is also a place for study of the scriptures and a location for community events.

The key place in the synagogue is arguably the Ark. It is in the Ark that the scrolls of the *Torah* are kept, often behind drawn curtains. The scrolls are wound around two wooden rods and kept in the Ark usually wrapped in velvet cloths. The *bimah* is the stand on which the *Torah* is read by the cantor or person who leads the prayers. A rabbi or teacher is the person who may preach a sermon from a pulpit, discussing some aspect of the *Torah*. The Ark is usually kept at the eastern side of the synagogue, facing in the direction of Jerusalem. Normally, the congregation can always see the Ark because of the arrangement of the seating.

In a traditional synagogue there is a gallery around three sides of the building in which women and girls sit, and who are hence separate from the men who participate in the prayers and the service. During the Saturday morning service, the *Torah* is taken out of the Ark and read from the *bimah*. The *Torah* may also be carried around the synagogue.

Originally, Judaism was a religion which involved sacrifice, and this was traditionally conducted at the Temple in Jerusalem. However, in 586 BCE, the Babylonian armies conquered Judah and many Jews were taken back to Babylonia. Like any people forcibly removed from their homeland, there was a preoccupation with sustaining their religion and customs, and it was during this period that the idea of the synagogue came into practice. Eventually, when in 538 BCE they were allowed to return home, ending the diaspora or dispersion, the function of the synagogue was well established.

see also...

Diaspora; Judaism; Sabbath

Talmud

The *Talmud* is a long collection of writings and commentaries on Judaism by rabbis. The first section of the *Talmud* is termed the *Mishnah*. Another major part is termed the *Gemara*. Other parts of the *Talmud* are the *Halachah* and the *Agadah*.

Although the *Torah* has scriptural authority in Judaism, nevertheless the interpretations of learned rabbis carry a great deal of respect. Their views were transmitted orally originally, but eventually they were committed to writing as the *Talmud*. The latter contains analyses and comments on such matters as the conduct of temple affairs and of religious ceremonies, on matters of hygiene, on questions of laws and their interpretation and on ethical issues.

The *Talmud* also contains succinct sayings and short statements of wisdom on a variety of matters. These can be amusing and provide down-to-earth comments on how people ought to cope with the trials and tribulations of everyday life. There are comments included in the *Talmud* from many hundreds of rabbis. These writings span a period of about 500 years from the first century CE to the fifth century CE. The writings of the *Talmud* can provide profound insights into the scriptures. They can enable people to remember a spiritual message in a concise form. They have the effect of being thought provoking and of helping people to reflect upon spiritual truths. The *Talmud* is an essential part of the curriculum for the education of rabbis.

Historically, two separate *Talmuds* were compiled. One is known as the *Palestinian* or *Jerusalem Talmud*, and the other as the *Babylonian Talmud*. They are both written in the same languages of Hebrew and Aramaic, but the *Babylonian Talmud* is longer.

see also...

Diaspora; Judaism; Synagogue; Torah

Tantrism

This is one of the oldest and most esoteric strands of thought in the Hindu, Jain and Buddhist traditions. The sources of Tantrism are partly some complex tantric texts, but, perhaps more importantly, the oral and practical teaching which is transmitted from guru to pupil.

The followers of Tantra have frequently, although not exclusively, been outside the organisation of orthodox religion. They have been mendicants or yoga adepts who followed practices and rituals which were frowned upon by members of mainstream Indian religion. Such practices may have involved the consumption of alcohol and meat, and unorthodox sexual rituals. The purpose of tantric practices is ultimately the same as mainstream Hinduism and Buddhism, that is, to attain union with the divine, to gain release from the cycle of rebirth, and to realise the true self.

Among the techniques characteristic of Tantra are the *yantra* and the mantra. The *yantra* is a mandala or cosmological diagram, which is used as the object of meditation. The purpose of such meditation is to look back in time and gain an understanding of the original creative process of the universe. The mantra, on the other hand, is a short series of sounds, which may or may not have a literal meaning, and which are intended to be repeated and intoned during meditation. Perhaps the most famous *yantra* is the *Shri Yantra*, and *om*, a well-known mantra.

The tantric tradition has been kept alive particularly through Tibetan Buddhism. However, the potent nature of the psychology involved, and the unconventional nature of the rituals, result in advice from practitioners that tantra should only be studied under the guidance of an experienced guru.

see also...

Hinduism; Mantra; Mysticism; Sadhu; Yoga

Taoism

Taoism is a mystical religious tradition which developed in China. The word 'tao', after which Taoism is named, may be translated as the 'way' or the 'truth'. Lao Tzu is considered to be the founder of Taoism, and he was born in approximately 600 BCE. Little is known of his life, but he wrote the *Tao Te Ching*, which is the principal text of Taoism.

A number of different meanings and interpretations may be attached to the concept of the *Tao*. It may be thought of as the source of energy which enables the universe to function; and in parallel to this interpretation, it may be considered as the way of life which best enables an individual human being to live in accord with this energy.

In perhaps its purist form Taoism encapsulates a mystical approach to nature, the world and the universe. The Taoist strives to exist in harmony with nature and in general terms does not see death as a terrible event. For the Taoist the world is full of opposites. Life and death are opposites, and are part of the inherent nature of the world. Hence

neither should have more attention attached to them than the other. As part of seeking to live in empathy with things, the Taoist does not try to enhance his or her own self-image at the expense of another. Taoists would generally adopt a self-effacing approach to life, and it seems totally in keeping with the philosophy of Taoism that we should know very little of the life of Lao Tzu. Perhaps this was deliberate, in that he did not seek to transmit details of his life.

The Taoist tries to attain a sense of harmony with nature by practising meditational techniques which have the effect of stilling and calming the mind. The Taoist aims at a psychological state where the mind is seeking nothing, and not striving all the time to attain something.

see also...

Buddhism

Theosophy

Theosophy is a broad-based philosophical and religious movement, whose central tenet is that it is possible to have a direct, mystical comprehension of the divine. One could well argue that there are theosophical trends and elements in many religious systems, but the term is normally associated with the Theosophical Society which was established in 1875. Although Theosophy has many elements integrated within it, there are some general themes which one can recognise as being theosophical.

Theosophy generally supports the notion that there is a single integrative spiritual force underlying all existence. The universe, and everything in it, is essentially a single entity. Theosophy has a traditional association with Hinduism and yogic systems, and with the attainment of some degree of influence over the material world.

Theosophy suggests that in the principal religions there is, first, a conventional, external practice composed perhaps of the principal festivals and the widely accepted modes of worship. Second, however, Theosophists suggest that there is an internal, mystical teaching within the principal religions, which emphasises a direct spiritual knowledge. Theosophists argue that this understanding may be obtained by such practices as meditation and the repetition of mantras or holy syllables.

The Theosophical Society was founded in the United States by Helena Blavatsky and Henry Olcott. The Society later moved the headquarters to Madras. Helena Blavatsky was the author of a famous work, *The Secret Doctrine*, which discussed Theosophical ideas. Theosophy does not claim to constitute a new world religion, but to synthesise mystical and spiritual principles which are present in the main world faiths.

see also...

Hinduism; Mysticism; Upanishads; Yoga

Tibetan Buddhism

The original religion of Tibet was known as Bon, and involved, among other aspects, the worship of nature. In the seventh century CE, however, King Srongtsen Gampo was converted to Buddhism, and he acted as a catalyst for the spread of Buddhism in Tibet. He was instrumental in developing an alphabet for the Tibetan language based on written Sanskrit. Tibetan Buddhism gradually developed, incorporating features of the Bon religion, of Hinduism and of teachings from the Tantras. The Buddhism of Tibet is sometimes known as Lamaism, since the senior religious figures are termed lamas. The senior lama is the Dalai Lama. Towards the end of the fifteenth century CE, a doctrine based on reincarnation developed whereby at death the soul of the senior lama was believed to transfer to a baby born at the time of death. The title of Dalai Lama (which translates as Ocean of Wisdom) is thus passed on through a system based on reincarnation.

When a Dalai Lama dies a search is conducted for the child who has received his soul. When identified the child is tested in various ways, including the recognition of possessions of the previous Dalai Lama. The present incumbent was born in 1935 and is the fourteenth Dalai Lama. He left Tibet in 1959 when the Chinese took over that country and now resides in northern India.

Tibet has produced a number of important religious figures, perhaps none more well known than Jetsun Milarepa. He was born in 1038 CE, near the Tibet–Nepal border. In middle age he studied under the guru Marpa and when his period of spiritual training was over, spent much of the rest of his life meditating in solitude in a mountain cave. A number of techniques are used in Tibetan Buddhism including the mantra or chanted syllable which is of religious significance. Used also are *yantras* and mandalas, religious diagrams often incorporating geometrical patterns.

see also...

Buddhism; Yoga

Torah

The *Torah* is part of the *Tenakh* or Jewish bible. The *Torah* contains five books: *Genesis, Exodus, Leviticus, Numbers* and *Deuteronomy*. The traditional origin of the *Torah* is traced back to the escape of the people of Israel from Egypt, and to the occasion in the Sinai desert when Moses climbed Mount Sinai to commune with God. It was during this period of prayer and meditation that it is assumed traditionally that God revealed the *Torah* to Moses, who then wrote it out. Jews believe that the *Torah* sets down the terms of God's covenant with the Jewish people and establishes the latter as the chosen of God.

The *Tenakh* is sometimes written as *TeNaKh*, as a partial acronym for the three main parts of the Bible. These are the *Torah*, or Law; the *Nevi'im*, or Prophets; and the *Ketuvim* or Writings. Originally these would have been passed on in an oral tradition, but eventually they were produced in written form.

The Orthodox Jewish perception of the *Torah* is that it is a final and complete revelation of God, and hence cannot and should not be altered in any way. In addition, each and every part of the *Torah* is regarded as just as significant as every other part. It is clear then that the *Torah* is at the theological heart of Judaism. Apart from its theological implications the *Torah* also embraces a history from creation to the end of the period of Moses. Scrolls of the *Torah* are usually inscribed by hand, and kept in the Ark in a synagogue.

The word 'torah' means teaching, and reflects God's covenant with the Jewish people. This covenant is regarded as clearly significant for Jews, but also significant for all other peoples. The Jews believe they were chosen as the vehicle through which God's teaching could be conveyed to all other human beings.

see also...

Covenant; Jerusalem; Judaism; Passover; Synagogue

Upanishads

The original religious texts of Hinduism are the *Vedas*. These can generally be thought of in two parts: the earlier is involved with procedures for sacrifice and religious ritual, while the later part deals with the mystical understanding of the nature of God. This latter element is termed the *Upanishads*. The meaning of 'upanishad' is 'to sit beside', indicating the disciple or devotee sitting at the feet of the guru, acquiring spiritual knowledge.

It is not entirely clear how many *Upanishads* were written originally, but 108 are still in existence. The essential message of the *Upanishads* is that there is a universal energy which is present everywhere, and which is the primal source of all things. This energy is called Brahman, and it is present also in the human soul. When men and women are aware of Brahman and live with Brahman in their consciousness, they are able to escape from the cycle of birth and death, and attain salvation. This message of the *Upanishads* is often summed up in the Sanskrit phrase, '*Tat tvam asi*' (you are that). It signifies that the individual is part of the universal soul.

According to the *Upanishads* the main purpose of life is to be united with Brahman, and anything which furthers that aim is laudable. Obsession with the self, and a preoccupation with material pleasures, are seen as hindering progress towards union with Brahman. The contemplative life is seen as of high value in that it is conducive to thinking about Brahman.

Some *Upanishads* are written in prose while some are written in verse or in a combination of the two. The names of the seers who wrote the *Upanishads* are unknown. The *Upanishads* are relatively uniform in their message and although they may differ somewhat in their form, the essential message of the relationship between the individual and the universal soul is contained in each one.

see also...

Hinduism; Mysticism

Vedas

The *Vedas* are the original sacred texts of Hinduism. They can be traced back to the second millennium BCE when the Aryan tribes who inhabited the southern Asian steppes developed a large number of hymns which expressed their relationship to the physical and spiritual world. These hymns were passed on by oral tradition, and their content became increasingly regularised, with the tribal priests ensuring that they were memorised and transmitted accurately from generation to generation. When the Aryans invaded India, the transmission of the hymns continued, and they were probably committed to writing in about 700 or 800 BCE.

The most significant of the collection of hymns is known as the *Rg Veda*. Other *Vedas* such as the *Sama*, *Yajur* and *Atharva Vedas* were produced later than the *Rg Veda*. The *Brahmanas* are later texts added to the *Vedas*, and the *Upanishads* are a subsection of the *Brahmanas*. All of these texts may be regarded as having a general religious cohesion. The *Rg Veda* mentions a great many gods. One of the most significant was Indra, the God of War. He was the god who, in a mythical sense, led the Aryan armies against their enemies. Agni was the God of Fire, and was important to priests because fire was used in the sacrificial ceremonies to the gods.

Mention is also made of Soma which is not only a deity but a drink prepared from a particular plant and used in the priestly ceremonies. It may be that *soma* was actually marijuana, since special psychological effects of the drink are noted. Varuna was the Vedic God who encouraged moral behaviour and when people did not behave according to His high moral standards, He punished them. Making sacrifices to the gods was very important in Vedic culture. The sacrifices were controlled by the priests, who had been schooled in the sacred texts.

see also...
Hinduism

Vishnu

ishnu is one of the three main gods of Hinduism: Brahma, Vishnu and Shiva. Vishnu is generally portrayed as a man with a deep-blue skin, and possessing four arms with which he is supposed to be able to reach throughout the universe. Vishnu's wife is the goddess Lakshmi, who is the Goddess of Wealth. She too has four arms, in two of which she is often shown carrying lotus flowers. Vishnu is often portrayed riding on Garuda, the eagle. Vishnu is seen as the creator of the universe and of everything in it. He is a very popular god, particularly in the form of his various incarnations.

Many Hindus follow either Vishnu or Shiva. Followers of the former are known as Vaishnavites, and of the latter Shaivites; although the two large traditions of devotion tend to exist together without any undue animosity. Vishnu is very much regarded as a kind and supportive deity.

Vishnu is particularly famous because of his incarnations, when He chose to take the form of a living being in order to achieve some specific good

purpose on earth. There have developed historically ten principal incarnations of Vishnu which are Matsya (the fish); Kurma (the tortoise); Varaha (the boar); Narasimha (the Man-lion); Vamana (the dwarf); Parasurama (Rama with an axe); Rama, as he appears in the *Ramayana*; Krishna; Buddha; and Kalkin, the myth of the incarnation of Vishnu to come in the future.

It is interesting that the Buddha is included as an *avatar* or incarnation of Vishnu. This probably demonstrates the tolerance of Hinduism towards other faiths, which has been demonstrated throughout history. Hinduism has tended to attempt to assimilate other religious ideas rather than to conflict with them. The best known *avatars* of Vishnu are probably Rama and Krishna.

see also...

Hinduism; Krishna; Sadhu; Sanskrit; Shiva

Vivekananda

Vivekananda (1863–1902) was an Indian religious leader and thinker who did a great deal to integrate traditional Hindu ideas with those of western materialism. He thought that the two traditions had a great deal to gain from each other.

Vivekananda's original name was Narendranath Datta and he was born in Calcutta in 1863. His family was wealthy and in addition to being educated in the eastern tradition, he also received tuition in European philosophy and science, and in Christianity. Despite his privileged background, he became preoccupied with the need for measures to help eradicate poverty in India and also to spread educational opportunities to the whole population.

He became a member of the society known as the Brahma Samaj, which was a Hindu Reformist movement which had been founded by Ram Mohan Ray. The organisation tended to reject the more mystical elements in Hinduism, and the more esoteric aspects of Hindu worship. It was very much concerned with the reform of society, and in particular in supporting such issues as education for poorer classes in society, and equal opportunities for women.

Vivekananda became a follower of the Bengali mystic Ramakrishna, and joined the Ramakrishna Mission. Ramakrishna espoused the doctrine that all of the major world religions pointed in the direction of the same truth. He was also devoted to social reconstruction and reform. Ramakrishna named Vivekananda as his successor within the Ramakrishna Mission. Vivekananda helped to establish the Ramakrishna *ashram* (monastery) at Calcutta in 1898. Vivekananda particularly espoused the teachings of Vedanta and was very much influential in extending the popularity of this philosophy in the West.

see also...

Hinduism

Worship

Worship is the process whereby a member of a particular faith expresses reverence for the deity of that religion, or of some important feature of the faith. It would perhaps be more normal to think of the use of the concept in relation to a god and to a theistic religion. Hence in Buddhism it may not be appropriate to think of Buddhists worshipping a statue of the Buddha, or worshipping the Buddhist teachings. It may be more accurate to say that they show great respect for the teachings and try to put them into practice.

Worship in religion has a variety of purposes. First, it enables the worshipper to pay homage and show reverence to the deity, and also enables a form of spiritual communication to take place. There are also often psychological benefits to worshippers, in that they feel more at peace, or perhaps feel that they have unburdened themselves of anxieties.

The process of worship may take place in several ways including the singing of hymns, prayer, meditation, chanting, and different religious rituals. Religious images often have a particular significance in worship. Some people find it much easier to worship if they have an image upon which to focus their attention. In Hinduism statues of gods and goddesses are very common in temples and are the focus of much reverence from worshippers. A statue may be treated very much as if it were a real person, i.e. 'dressing' and 'feeding' it in the morning and then putting it to bed in the evening. In Christianity the image of Jesus Christ suffering upon the cross is a very potent image, which helps Christians to focus upon some of the key themes of Christ's message. Not all religions approve the use of images in worship, however. One example is Islam: Muslims are strongly opposed to images of Allah, feeling that this is completely counter to the concept of Allah.

see also...

Christianity; Hinduism; Islam

Yoga

Within classical Hinduism, yoga was one of the methods for achieving salvation or release from the perpetual cycle of reincarnation. The word is derived from the same source as the word 'yoke'. The yoking or joining in this spiritual sense refers to the merging of the individual with the universal spirit or *Brahman*.

It is Hatha yoga, with its system of physical postures (*asanas*) and breathing exercises which have made yoga well known outside India. However, yoga is a more comprehensive system than that simply of physical exercises. It involves meditative processes for both calming and focusing the mind; and the practice of non-violence or *ahimsa*, which besides not engaging in aggressive or unpleasant words and actions, may also involve vegetarianism as a means of not killing animals for food.

Yoga may also involve a systematic attempt to avoid responding to sense perceptions. By this is meant that the student of yoga tries not to see objects or people as attractive or unattractive, and tries not to wish for things, or to wish to avoid things. In other words the yogi attempts to be calm in the face of whatever sense perceptions may arise.

In the *Bhagavad Gita*, Krishna advises Arjuna that there are two principal methods of yoga, *jnana yoga* or the pursuit of wisdom, and *karma yoga* or the pursuit of action which is devoted to God. Krishna advocates the latter as a means of acquiring wisdom. He suggests that people can never truly avoid acting in a social context, but that they should never become attached to the potential results of their actions. In this way their actions will have a purity which otherwise would be lacking. Krishna stresses that the yogi should not have desires and wishes concerning the world, for the world of the senses does not bring lasting happiness.

see also...

Bhagavad Gita; Hinduism

Zen

Zen is a variant of Buddhism which developed in Japan, and which reflects much of the culture of that country. The term 'zen' is derived from a Sanskrit word for meditation, which occupies a central position in Zen practice. Communal meditation is a very important feature of the Zen monastic discipline, although there are two broad schools which tend to adopt a different focus.

The Rinzai school, started by Eisai, often teaches by using the technique of the *koan*. This is an apparently confusing short saying, deliberately structured in order to resist rational or logical analysis. An often quoted example is, 'What is the sound of one hand clapping?' The novice monk is given, by the *roshi* or abbot of the monastery, a personal *koan* on which to contemplate and try to resolve. The monk may be asked to make the *koan* the subject of meditation sessions. Periodically the *roshi* will ask to see the novice for a personal interview, to explore whether progress has been made in its resolution.

However, the Soto school, started by Dogen, teaches by using rather more traditional Buddhist techniques. The monks and nuns practise using long periods of sitting meditation, during which they try to calm the mind, and eliminate the constant flow of thoughts and attachments. The novices try to remain very focused on the present moment, but without engaging in reflective thought. The ultimate goal of novices in both schools is enlightenment or *satori*. Almost by definition this is a mystical experience for which words are inadequate. However, as an approximation, it is said to be a state in which one is able to live fully consciously and sensitively aware of one's present existence, yet without attempting to want anything or become anything. One simply lives in the fullest and most sensitive manner of which a human is capable.

see also...

Buddhism

Zoroastrianism

Zoroastrianism is the ancient religion of Iran (Persia) and still retains a few adherents in that country, and, in a culturally modified form, in India. In about 1500 BCE a group of migrating nomads from the southern Asian steppes settled in northern Persia. At about this period a prophet arose whose name was Zarathustra or Zoroaster. He was believed by his followers to be able to reveal the teaching of God.

Zoroaster taught, in particular, that each person had a degree of individual responsibility for his or her own religious and spiritual thoughts. People are confronted all the time with ethical dilemmas, and must try to do good and refrain from doing evil. Heaven awaited those who acted morally, while evildoers would go to hell. To some extent this approach to spirituality was undermining the power of the traditional priests since lay individuals did not need the intercession of a priest.

Zoroastrianism became the established religion of Persia and the Persian empire until the Muslim invasion of Persia in 633 CE. After that time there were gradual attempts to replace Zoroastrianism by Islam as the religion of the people. Islam gradually took over as the majority faith, and today there are only relatively small numbers of Zoroastrians remaining, largely in remote rural communities. In the tenth century a group of Zoroastrians left Persia to settle in India, because of the conflict with Islam, and became the Parsi community.

Although Zoroastrians believe in heaven and hell, they do not regard being sent to hell as being for eternity. The real purpose of hell is to try to help human beings reform themselves, and then to move to resting with God. Zoroastrians do not reject the material world, but, in fact, regard it as essentially good and noble, since it is the creation of God.

see also...

Parsi

Further reading

Cupitt, D. (1997) *After God*. London, Weidenfeld & Nicolson.

Hinnells, J.R. (1996) *Zoroastrians in Britain*. Oxford, Oxford University Press.

Keown, D. (1996) *A Very Short Introduction to Buddhism*. Oxford, Oxford University Press.

McLeod, W.H. (1968) *Guru Nanak and the Sikh Religion*. Oxford, Clarendon Press.

Pye, M. (1979) *The Buddha*. London, Duckworth.

Robertson, J. (1999) *Windows to Eternity*. Oxford, Bible Reading Fellowship.

Saddhatissa, H. (1970) *Buddhist Ethics*. London, Allen & Unwin.

Shillington, V.G. (ed.) (1997) *Jesus and His Parables*. Edinburgh, T. and T. Clark.

Smart, N. (ed.) (1992) *The World's Religions*. Cambridge, Cambridge University Press.

Suzuki, D.T. (1969) *An Introduction to Zen Buddhism*. London, Rider.

Thompson, M. (1997) *Philosophy of Religion*. London, Hodder Headline.

Unterman, A. (1981) *Jews: Their Religious Beliefs and Practices*. London, Routledge.

Watt, W.M. (1985) *Islamic Philosophy and Theology*. Edinburgh, Edinburgh University Press.

Zaehner, R.C. (1966) *Hinduism*. Oxford, Oxford University Press.

Zaehner, R.C. (ed.) (1988) *Encyclopedia of Living Faiths*. London, Hutchinson.

Also available in the series